IT HAPPENED IN PICKENS COUNTY

BY

PEARL SMITH McFALL

PUBLISHED BY

THE SENTINEL PRESS

PICKENS, SOUTH CAROLINA

ABOUT THE AUTHOR

Mrs. Pearl Smith McFall has been collecting local history for twenty-five years, through D.A.R. work and other research.

In 1953 she wrote a book called **"So Lives The Dream"** which is a history of the old Pendleton District and the beginning of Clemson College.

Mrs. McFall is a member of the South Carolina D.A.R., and the Carolina Piedmont Branch of the National League of American Pen Women. She studied Journalism at Columbia University in New York City a few years ago.

The present book, **"It Happened In Pickens County"** is an accumulation of facts and traditional stories she has collected through the years.

CONTENTS

Addendum—Sketch of Table Rock—
By Mrs. Nettie C. Sutherland

Appendix—List of County Officers

Acknowledgements

Index

Picture Section

Chapter One.

Traditionally speaking the first white men to set foot on Pickens County soil were DeSoto and his band of Spanish explorers in 1540, just forty-eight years after Columbus discovered America. History tells us that DeSoto was well equipped to deal ruthlessly with native savages when he set out on his expedition from Mexico.

His route has caused controversy. Some historians claim that he led his band through the Georgia mountains and then westward. Others say they visited North and South Carolina, and Tennessee. There are indications that they visited all of these places and lingered in the Carolina mountains a number of years.

Historians agree that the word "Chalaque" in Hernando DeSoto's notes was a Spanish attempt at the word Cherokee.

James Mooney, widely recognized historian of early American and Indian life says DeSoto and his men marched from Cofitachiqui (Silver Bluff, Georgia) to the head waters of Keowee River. And Keowee River is in Pickens County, South Carolina. Afterwards they probably turned northeast across the Saluda, Tyger, and Pacolet Rivers along an old Indian Trail (or path).

Those early Indian Trails had been made by buffaloes and other heavy animals tramping through the forest to watering places and grazing lands, and tribes of Indians following the same routes.

Did Pickens County have buffaloes? Yes. And thousands of deer. (Ref: Adair, Mooney, Lawson, Hewitt). "Upper South Carolina."

The stories of DeSoto coming this way persisted for

centuries without further proof than a few half forgotten notes in very old histories, and then in 1935 a farmer near Inman, South Carolina (a little town northwest of Spartanburg) plowed up a queer shaped stone in his field. It was no Indian relic because Indians were uneducated. This stone bears the date 1567 in Roman Numerals and a parallelogram which could have suggested a fort, and a symbol of the sun with an arrow pointing.

The stone was sent to Washington and reliable authorities decided it was possibly a sign on the old Indian Trail indicating a day's journey to Fort San Juan, which was supposed to have existed somewhere in this section.

From time immemorial the Carolina mountains were inhabited by Indians. We read of Iriquois, Shawnees, Choctaws, Creeks, Senecas, Catawabas, Chickasaws, and Cherokees that passed this way. Adair frequently mentions the earlier tribes as living in wigwams. But the Cherokees seem to have adopted some of the ideas of civilization and when our first white settlers came to Pickens County most of them were living in crude log cabins.

There were three types of white men who came to upper South Carolina, after the Spaniards, before the first white homesteaders. These were the adventurers who have been called "Hunters." The next were known as "Cow Drivers." They were a crude sort of ranchmen who set up a form of cattle raising in the luxuriant pasture lands that the Hunters had told them about. And next came the "Traders," at first free-lance traders and later traders who were licensed by the government.

Geographically, there were three divisions of Cherokee Indians. The "Otarre" (Lower Hill Cherokees) living in the mountains that are now Pickens and Oconee County, the Middle Cherokees in North Carolina, and the "Ayrate" (Over Hill Cherokees) in what is now east Tennessee.

James Adair lived with the Chickasaw and Cherokee Indians for forty years. His history of the American Indians was published in London in 1775. He spoke several languages and was well versed in Indian dialects. One point that he stresses all through his history is his belief that the American Indians are descendants of the lost tribes of Israel. He said that Indians possessed in beautiful form certain elements of literature, religion and philosophy. But he also told much of their cruelty.

The Cherokees had never heard of Christ but they believed in a "Great Spirit" who governed the Universe and lived in the winds and clouds. They believed strange things about animals and nature, but in their natural state they tried to conform to certain standards that would please the "Great Spirit." They believed in some kind of future life. The good went to the "Happy Hunting Ground," and the bad to a land of horrors.

The early white settlers in Pickens County, as elsewhere, feared the Indians on account of their strange customs and had little patience with them. If they had treated them as human beings instead of savages the Indian history of America might have been different. But it is understandable that they couldn't realize that. And the savages grew worse as whiskey traffic increased.

One of the strange customs of the American Indians from Mexico to the Great Lakes was their fear and seeming reverence of the rattlesnake. They would not kill one and if a trader or other stranger in their midst killed one they almost certainly punished him for it. And the usual form of punishment was what they called a "dry scratch." They had a small curry comb made of snakes' teeth and with that they would scratch the blood out of the man's bare back. They did this to ward off the evil that the snake might do to them. For he was a devil incarnate, whom they recognized as the king of all nature.

James Mooney, at one time Secretary of the Colony of

South Carolina, began exploring the mountains of this section about 1690. He lived among the Cherokees to study them. He learned their games and pastimes, their dances, and ceremonial occasions. He learned the meaning of the musical sounding names they gave the streams and villages. Many of these are familiar to us today: Keowee, Oolenoy, Eastatoe. Secona, Saluda, Cateechee, Isaqueena, and many others. Even our Blue Ridge Mountains were called by an Indian word that meant the "Great Blue Hills of God," and the white men shortened it to "Blue Ridge."

The Cherokee Indians lived in villages. It is impossible to locate the sites of all the villages for the smaller ones moved from place to place to be nearer good hunting grounds. The Cherokees always selected a place on the banks of a stream for the convenience of having water nearby for family use, for the easy fishing that most of our streams afforded in that day, and for the patches of valley land along the streams which the Indian women cultivated with their stone and wooden tools.

They raised corn, beans, pumpkins, squashes, tobacco. and gourds (for dippers and containers). In summer they gathered huckleberries, blackberries, grapes, plums, and other wild fruit. And sometimes they found "bee" trees in the woods that provided honey for sweetening. The men hunted and fished for their supply of meat. The woods were full of deer and bear and smaller animals.

There were important Cherokee villages that did not change their location until the Indians were moved west. Keowee Village on the West bank of Keowee River was one of these. The spot is in Oconee County now, but for a long time it was in Pickens District. It is not our intention to infringe on the history of other counties, but to clarify certain points it will be necessary to include some the background that belongs to both counties. And Keowee Village was the principal town for all of this area.

It extended along the river bank for some distance, a single line of cabins and wigwams. The "Town House" which was the focal point of every important Indian village stood on a mound near the center of the village and was surrounded by an open square of several acres. The square had been leveled and sanded for a chungke yard, and it was used for a ball field and for ceremonial dances that took place on state occasions.

Chungke was the Cherokee's National Sport. It was played with polished stones similar in shape to a Greek discus. Two players at a time threw the stones toward a center pole and ran after them with long poles trying to prevent each other from touching the stone before it reached its goal. It took speed and dexterity to win the game by touching a stone the greatest number of times.

The Town House was built of logs placed up and down with canes laced in between them in a latticed effect. It had a thatched roof of grass and clay. It was large enough to seat two or three hundred people. It had a pit in the center of the big room to hold the sacred fire for ceremonial occasions. Visiting Chiefs and Councilmen sat around this fire in a circle. There was no chimney to take off the smoke and ventilation came from the open door and the cracks in the walls. If a meeting was at night the brightly burning fire and pine flares furnished the illumination.

Cherokees never seemed to mind the smoky atmosphere but it was very unpleasant to white men. Some of the cabins had a lean-to back room with a fire pit for warmth in winter. This was for the comfort of old people and children. The active men and women spent most of their time in the outdoors and were hardened to weather conditions.

Cherokees did not have many children, usually two or three to a family. Like Orientals, the Cherokees reverenced the old people of their tribes and took special care of them.

From earliest times Cherokees were divided into seven

clans. This would not mean much to us but it meant a great deal to them and was probably a safeguard against incest. No Indian boy was allowed to take a maiden for his wife who belonged to the same clan. But when a Cherokee married (no matter what the marriage ceremony, or lack of it) they remained faithful and the children became members of the wife's clan.

The clans identified themselves by some decoration or head dress and loyalty was the watchword of each clan. If a Cherokee was killed the members of his clan were ready to take "an eye for an eye, a tooth for a tooth," and thy would go a hundred miles to get somebody's scalp if he had wronged a member of their clan. This often brought on Indian wars, and then the whole Cherokee Nation (or their particular part of the Nation) was ready to help.

There was no absolute governing body in the Cherokee Nation. Some of the older Chiefs had a great deal of influence if they had been cited for bravery in wars, or distinguished themselves in some way. These men from "Overhill," "Middle," and "Lower Hill" tribes attended important Council Meetings in each other's villages. Each village was a law unto itself with all adults, even the women, having a voice in the management of affairs.

The women of each clan selected a clan group in a Tribe. These were called the "Womens' Council". Then they selected the most outstanding woman in their group for the "Council Leader" and she was known as the "Beloved Woman." This Beloved Woman had great power among them for they believed that the Great Spirit spoke to them through her. These Beloved Women have been known to save the lives of white settlers many times in the passing years.

Some writers have pictured Indian women as down-trodden drudges afraid to move or speak in the presence of their savage husbands. That was not true. In those early years before the white men came and filled the Cherokee men with antagonism, and corn whisky, they seem to have been good husbands. It is all in the point of view.

The women cooked, worked in the fields and gardens, and made buckskin garments and feathered head dresses for the head men and women. The children went nude in summer, but the big boys and men wore breech cloths. The women wore loose garments, sometimes tied around the waist with leather thongs, or a fringed buckskin belt.

But their lives were not all work. They found congenial women friends and wove rugs and blankets together. They made artistic baskets of grasses and honeysuckle vines, and heavier ones of white oak splints for gathering the field produce. They often made plates and pots of the mountain clay that was plentiful along the streams. They willingly accepted their work as a fair division of the family labor. They loved the wild flowers, and the trees and plants in the woods. Each of these spoke to them in its own language as a symbol of something they could understand. Few women of our Garden Clubs today will ever know our native plants as well as they did. They had unfailing remedies for everything. If herbs did not cure them they used the "Bezoar or madstone" sometimes found in deer.

They knew the bark and roots that would make the necessary colors of dye for their rugs and blankets. From generation to generation the medicinal value of plants had been passed down to them and there was little sickness among them. The historian Adair said he had never seen an Indian die from a snake bite because they always had the proper remedy at hand. They loved the birds and animals and told their children fantastic legends about them—legends that are comparable with the mythology of our oldest Nations.

The way our native Cherokees lived might not mean much to Christian men and women of today but to those whose ashes rest in Indian mounds in the soil of Pickens County it was a full and complete life. "Without money and without price" they lived and moved and had their being as best they could according to their standards and opportunities.

The men of the tribes hunted and fished to supply their families with meat. They made canoes to travel on the rivers to better hunting grounds. They made tools of wood and stone, for they were just emerging from the stone age when America was discovered. They made war clubs, bows and arrows, and shields. They made untold numbers of arrowheads and carved beautiful peace-pipes to smoke on State occasions. They trained their boy children with small bows and arrows to shoot at grasshoppers.

Indians have often been described as stern and always savage, but in their own environment they were goodnatured, enjoying games and pastimes. War was the only excitement they knew, and to be able to tread the warpath at some time was the ambition of every young brave.

Each village had a War Chief and a Peace Chief. In times of peace the War Chief remained in the background, but when trouble came he was ready to take command. The annual hunting season which came in the late fall often brought on war with other tribes. Many disputes arose over hunting grounds. The Cherokees sometimes traveled far on their hunting trips and Creeks and Catawbas declared war when they came into their territory.

When the War Chief desired his men to march against an enemy he would march three times around the war cabin where they kept their war paint, bows and arrows, beating a drum and sounding the war whoop. The braves and warriors would quickly gather around him. He would tell them his reasons for wanting to fight and remind them of the Cherokees' tribal pride and past valor. They must uphold the courage of their race.

After a ceremonial dance they would retire to the Town House for a period and drink black tea made from a certain evergreen tree, which was supposed to insure them life in battle. Then they donned paint and feathers and went shouting down the Trail, with their War Chief leading the way. At first they went single file but after they had gained the deep forest they slipped from tree to tree and moved silently as they approached the enemy. As stealthy as wild beasts they pounced upon their prey and brought back many scalps which they painted inside with red paint and hung in their war cabin. Sometimes they brought prisoners who could be used at various duties around the village.

The War Chief was held responsible if he lost a number of his men. They claimed that his impurity was responsible for his bad luck and he was degraded and his post of honor given to another brave warrior.

In peace time the Cherokees carried on considerable commerce by canoes on the rivers and along their Trails. They used the barter system and exchanged skins and furs, pottery and baskets for a fine quality of flint from Ohio for making arrow-heads, and for red sandstone from Minnesota that made beautiful pipes. Perhaps the Seneca Indians who had a village "Esenaka" close by our bridge over the Seneca River near the present Clemson College brought the first of these things South.

Soon after that James Mooney and other explorers went back to old Charles Town and Savannah telling about the wealth of our mountain country, white traders started bringing pack horses loaded with bright baubles to trade to Indians for valuable skins and furs. Sometimes they would bring knives and guns, and tin pans and bright cloth, and beads the women adored. But they never brought merchandise of equal value with the things they took back. They would put bells on their horses and come jingling through the forest to the delight of the Cherokees. The men were wild about horses. They had never seen horses until the explorers and traders came, and would pay any price for one, or steal them when they could. And this was the way our valley called "Horse-pasture" got its name. It was a safe hiding place for Indians' stolen horses and it wasn't many miles from Keowee Village. The Cherokees had no scruples about stealing. They didn't know any better. Before the white men came everything had been free and they took what they wanted.

Eastatoe was the next largest Indian village in this section, after Keowee. It was located in what we now call Eastatoe Valley where two streams come together, and we are told that it had about two hundred cabins and wigwams. There were several ancient mounds close by in the shadow of the heavily wooded mountains. When a trader asked one of the old Indian Chiefs who built them, he replied they had been there since "time out of mind." None of the mounds in Pickens County have been opened but just across the Georgia line some similar looking mounds have been opened by the Smithsonian Institute. They proved to be small pyramids that had been used by the Indians as tombs for hundreds of years, layer on layer.

In the Cherokee language "Eastatoe" meant "Place of Green Birds." A small green bird was used as the emblem of this tribe. It is supposed to be the "Carolina Parokeet," which is almost extinct.

Jocassee was a beautiful Indian maiden, the daughter of a Chief, who drowned herself when her father hindered her from marrynig the brave she loved. Perhaps her lover came from a member of the same clan in another tribe, or perhaps the Chief had his heart set on another son-in-law. But when he came and told her that her lover was dead she jumped into the river from the canoe where she was sitting and was drowned.

Those who have keen eyes and a lively imagiantion can sometimes see her canoe drifting in the shadows of the trees along the river bank on moonlight nights, or hear a distant Indian love call as they walk through the forest.

The "Green Corn Festival" was one of the great annual celebrations of the Cherokees. It came at the seventh moon of the year, which was in September. It was really a great thanksgiving service that lasted a week or more. All of the Cherokee families came, from the small villages to the largest one in their community, to take part in it. It was their way of expressing thanks to the "Great Spirit" for the corn and meat and personal blessings of the past year. All enemies in their tribe were forgiven. The fires were extinguished and new fires were started by Adwehi (the wise man of the tribe). This was to consecrate each home to the service of the Great Spirit. Those who had grown good crops brought bags of corn or other produce and deposited them at the Town House for their less fortunate neighbors, as a symbol of the first fruits of their labors. They feasted together and played all of the Indian games. And while the men played ball and chungke, and the young people gathered in great crowds to watch them, the mothers and grandmothers learned new designs of weaving from each other.

King George I, who was on the throne of England at that time, heard many stories of the natural wealth of the Cherokee country and began sending emissaries to investigate. They learned that the French people were also becoming interested.

In 1721 Sir Frances Nicholson, the first Royal Governor of the Province of South Carolina, sent delegates to invite the head Chiefs of the "Lower Hill" Cherokees to come to a Council Meeting at old Charles Town. The Indians went, and some of them were from what is now Pickens County. While they were in Charles Town they made a treaty with the white men by which a tract of land, about fifty square miles between Santee, Edisto and Saluda, was ceded to the English. This was their first land cession in South Carolina. There was no Indian village in the ceded section, and the hunting was not good. They probably considered the land worthless.

Nine years later, in 1730, Sir Alexander Cummings was sent from England to travel among the Cherokees. His party landed at old Charles Town and procured an interpreter named William Cooper to travel with them to the "back country." They followed the old Keowee Indian Trail which passed through our present county, crossed the road we now travel to Walhalla, went behind the present Gap Hill Church, and on to Keowee Village.

It was springtime. Hundreds of white dogwoods were blooming among the evergreen pine and hemlock trees. The mountains, plainly visible from hilltops, were very blue. Fish were jumping in the clear mountain streams, and the men often surprised deer or flocks of wild turkeys along the way. It was a beautiful land and bore signs of untold resources. Sir Alexander Cummings decided to claim it for the King of England.

Word passed among the Cherokees that white men were coming. They did not have pack horses laden with trinkets. They were not traders. Two or three hundred Cherokees gathered at the Town House and waited, more curious than hostile.

Armed with pistols and a sword under his flowing coat Sir Alexander Cummings marched proudly into the Town House. The interpreter, William Cooper, was quaking with fear. No one, not even the Cherokees themselves, ever carried arms into the Town House. But perhaps Sir Alexander's friendly attitude and his manner of assurance won them. He soon convinced the Chiefs that the English people were their friends.

The meeting lasted all day and before it was over he had persuaded the Council, through his interpreter, to send for all the leading Chiefs of the Middle and Overhall Tribes that they might form a lasting agreement of friendship.

Apparently convinced by the fascinating personality of this strange white man, the Indians dispatched runners to the Overhill and Middle Tribes for the Chiefs to meet in fifteen days at Nequasse (an Indian town near the present Franklin, N. C.) to discuss the agreement.

The interpreter was even more astounded. "Had I know what Sir Alexander Cummings would require me to say to those Cherokees I would never have dared to go into their Town House", he said. And he watched with interest and amazement the increasing friendship and the development of the daring exploit which had started at Keowee Village in South Carolina. The agreement was completed at Nequasse at the alloted time and seven Indian Chiefs finally agreed to go back to England with Sir Alexander to visit the king.

The youngest Indian in the party of Chiefs was Atta-kulla-kulla of Keowee Village. After the trip to Charles Town the boat trip to England took a month, and the Indians stayed in England four months. They visited the King and met his family. The splendor of the Court amazed them. They had never seen such sights nor heard such sounds. Attakulla-kulla was more impressed than any of the others, perhaps because of his youth. The words of the agreement they made with the King stayed with him all his life and he often repeated them to his people.

King George I fastened an imaginary chain to the breast of the head Chief, and the other end to his own breast and said: "This chain must always remain bright and new. It must never be allowed to grow rusty."

After the Cherokees were at home again treading the familiar Indian paths in our Carolina mountains Attakulla-kulla became a Peace Chief and he often traveled to Council Meetings among the Middle and Overhill Tribes trying to influence his people to remain loyal to the King of England, "The Great White Father."

The site of Keowee Indian Village is marked by a bronze plate on a boulder that rests on a barren hillside above Keowee River. Probably the same mound where the Town House once stood in the shadow of our Blue Ridge Mountains. It has been more than 200 years since the Cherokees roamed through Pickens County, but they left us a heritage of beautiful place names. *"Insundiga"* and *"Kulsage"* are two we have never used.

Chapter Two

Fort Prince George was erected in 1753 in gun-shot distance of the Indian Village Keowee, directly across the river. It was designed to be a much more formidable structure than the ordinary stockade enclosures that had been built in many places for the protection of white settlers.

It was built in the form of a square, with a rampart or wall of earth about six feet in height on which stockades were fixed. A ditch and natural glasis strengthened two sides of it, and strong bastions the angles upon which were mounted sixteen small cannon—four on each bastion. Its barracks were sufficiently large for one hundred men.

War was brewing between France and England and each Nation felt a greedy interest in the rich fur trade that England had established with the Cherokees. Since the visit of Attakulla and the other Chiefs to England, twenty years before this, a strong bond of loyalty had existed between the Lower Hill Cherokees and King George, "the Great White Father." But the French were trying to connect a chain of trade with the Indians from Canada to the Mississippi River. They had made their way into North Carolina and claimed the "French Broad River," and "Herbert's Spring" at the head waters of Tugaloo, which they assured the Indians was magic water that would save them in battle if they drank from it.

Governor James Glenn of South Carolina decided that a back country fort manned with British soldiers would help to keep Britain's prestige before them. Transporting cannon, and other guns and ammunition from Charlestown, as well as many supplies to keep a garrison of soldiers, was a long and tedious ordeal, for the things had to be brought on pack-horses, but it was finally accomplished. The fort was named for George II, the son of King George 1st and called "Fort

Prince George." It was in Pickens County. Gov. Glenn made a formal purchase with the Cherokees for the land on which it was built, the first land deal in Pickens County.

Capt. Lachlan McIntosh was the first officer in charge of the fort. He managed his men well and treated the Indians kindly. He did not allow his men to loiter in Keowee Village and for a while it seemed that the fort would serve the purpose for which it was intended. He held the confidence of the Cherokees and they gave him no trouble. Many viistors from Charlestown came to the fort and reported on these visits in old histories.

The famous physician and naturalist, Dr. Alexander Garden came. He roamed the woods of "horsepasture" unmolsted by the Indians and sought new and strange plants and specimens of rock. He took some of the white mountain clay to England and had a tea-set made at one of the famous potteries, which he said was as fine as any he had ever seen from India. He was the man for whom the flower "Gardenia" was named.

At intervals the garrison at Fort Prince George changed places with the men at Star Fort. And that was the way that Allen Francis from Star Fort met and fell in love with the Indian maiden "Cateechee of Keowee."

The girl's real name was "Issaqueena" and she was a Creek Indian who had been captured in war and brought back to Keowee Village.

The beginning of the romance is lost in obscurity but the story has been told many times of a planned uprising against Fort Prince George, and how Cateechee made the trip to Star-Fort to warn her lover Allen Francis and the other English soldiers stationed there. Dr. J. Walter Daniel and some other historians of an earlier day say that Cateechee named our places and streams that are called by numerals, such as —One Mile Creek, Six Mile Mountain, Twelve Mile River, Eighteen, Twenty-three, Twenty-six, and on to Ninety-six

22

at Star-Fort. Other historians of more practical minds say it would have been impossible for an uneducated Indian maiden to have called these places by numbers. They think the early traders and explorers named them.

In 1759 Lieutenant Richard Cotymore was sent to replace McIntosh as the chief officer at Fort Prince George and the change was not good. Cotymore was unkind to the Indians and always acted very superior with them. He allowed his men to loaf a great deal in the village of Keowee. All of them drank and they brought rum to the Indian men and forced themselves upon the women and young girls.

By this time the traders had been forbidden to bring whisky to the Indians, it made them so wild, but the English soldiers seemed to be a law unto themselves. With this the trouble began. Parties of young warriors took to the field. It made no difference to them that innocent white persons were ruthlessly murdered. White men were their enemies and they must have revenge.

Lt. Cotymore dispatched a messenger to Charlestown to inform Governor Lyttleton that the Cherokees had gone on the warpath. And he ordered the commanders of the militia to collect their men and march to the Congarees (fort near present Columbia) where he would join them and go to Fort Prince George.

Word always traveled to the Cherokees, and when they heard of the Governor's decision to bring an army against their people they summoned thirty-two of their head chiefs and went to Charlestown to confer with Governor Lyttleton before he set out on his journey. They were earnestly trying to prevent trouble.

Lyttleton assured them that he had made up his mind to go to Fort Prince George and see for himself but since they had come to him as friends he would allow the chiefs to march back with his army. He would see that "not a hair of their heads was harmed." They were allowed to march with his

army to the Congarees, and when several hundred militia-
men joined them there the Indians were put in chains. They
marched the balance of the way with undying hatred in their
hearts. And when they reached Fort Prince George they were
shut up in a hut that was hardly large enough for six men.
And this was in Pickens County. Indian hatred was being nu-
tured by the white men.

The militia was not a disciplined army. They soon grew
discontented and many of them were afraid of the Indians
they could see lurking in the shadows. The Governor was
advised to send for Attakulla-kulla, the wisest chief in the
Cherokee nation. He was visiting other tribes.

He came immediately and listened to the long, threat-
ening speech that Governor Lyttleton made him. Then he
replied—that he had always been a warm friend of the
English, that he had helped to make the treaties with them
in Britain many years ago. He said that some of the young
Cherokee warriors who recently went to Virginia to help the
English fight the French had suffered unjustly by English
hands, and then they had returned to the village of Keowee
to find that their homes were being desecrated by English
soldiers. They had burned with rage, but, afraid to attack
the armed garrison at the fort, they had spent their vengance
on innocent white settlers.

Attakulla-kulla requested the release of three chiefs
among the imprisoned Indians to help round up the real of-
fenders. Occonostota of the "Overhills," Fiftoe of Keowee
Village, and the head warrior of Eastatoe Village were re-
released. According to the agreement between Attakulla-kulla
and Governor Lyttleton the other imprisoned Indians were
to be released as soon as these men could round up twenty-six
guilty warriors. Only three Indians were ever turned in and
Governor Lyttleton required them to be carried to Charlestown in irons where they met a horrible death. The other
chiefs imprisoned at Fort Prince George were brought out by
the garrison and ruthlessly murdered one by one. But that

was after Governor Lyttleton left to go back to Charlestown. Smallpox had broken out among the militia and spread into several Indian villages and the Cherokees were terrified. They had never had contagious diseases before and they believed that evil spirits were at work among them. Many of them drank the juices of poisonous plants or drowned themselves.

Occonostota of the Overhills, who was one of the chiefs that Attakulla-kulla had caused to be released, was very bitter about the whole experience. He had gone to Charlestown with the other chiefs in an effort to make a peaceful settlment with Governor Lyttleton and arrange for punishment of their savage warriors. His racial pride had been crushed by the humiliating and painful treatment he had received. He was a chieftain of great influence among the Cherokees. He gathered a strong party of warriors and surrounded Fort Prince George hoping to keep the garrison imprisoned until they would release the chiefs they were holding. After sevral days when the garrison had remained within the fort unimpressed by his warriors he resorted to strategy.

The Indians appeared to disband and scatter but he had instructed a group of them to hide in a thicket nearby. Then he sent a squaw from Keowee Village, who was always welcomed by the men at the fort, with a message to Cotymore to meet him down near the river for a conference.

Apparently without suspicion Cotymore and two other officers, Bell and Foster, walked down the path. Occonostota was standing on the other side of Keowee River with a bridle in his hands. He said that he had decided to go to Charlestown again to talk with the Governor about releasing his comrades and he wanted a white man to go with him. If Cotymore would promise him an escort he would go and catch the horses.

The minute Cotymore agreed to this Ossnostota flung the bridle around his head three times as a signal to his ambushed warriors. They killed Cotymore and wounded the other two men. And then the garrison came from the fort and murdered the Indian hostages who were still imprisoned.

Every warrior in all of the Cherokee villages was ready to go to war then. King George III had come to the throne of England by that time. They still thought of the King as the "Great White Father" He was something apart, but these white devils among them were something they must exterminate. They painted themselves in the most formidable manner, and arrayed with every instrument of death in their possession, they visited one white settlement after another.

Some of the white families heard of their plans and escaped by hiding in the woods until they had passed. Some starved, and some lived on roots and berries until they could find their way across rivers to other white settlements. The Keith family of the Oolenoy section have always told the traditional story of their ancestor "Cornelius Keith, Sr.", and his wife who hid in a cave and lived on berries until they could escape.

William Henry Lyttleton, who had helped to bring on the Indian trouble, was appointed Governor of Jamaica and William Bull became Governor of South Carolina. He applied to North Carolina and Virginia for help to subdue the Indians and it was about that time that some of the Pickens, Anderson and others who later became famous in upper South Carolina moved to the Long Cane section of Abbeville County. Andrew Pickens, for whom our town and County was named, was a young lad at that time.

In April 1760 seven troops of rangers were organized to protect frontier families and to keep the Cherokee Indians from going farther down in the State of South Carolina. Col. Montgomery and Capt. Grant were in charge of this expedition which led to Fort Prince George. (Ramsey's History 1809).

'They reached a place called Twelve Mile River (certainly in Pickens County), and proceeded in the night to surprise the Eastatoe Indian Village, about twenty miles from their camp. They burned the village of two hundred

26

wig-wams and cabins to ashes and the next day they destroyed all of the surrounding crops."

All of the smaller villages were razed to the ground. Looking back over a period of two hundred years it seems that both the whites and Indians were to blame, but some of the white men were not heartless. In one of the very old histories we found these words: "We saw the tracks of barefoot Indian children in the corn rows as we destroyed their crops and wondered if we were leaving them to starve."

About sixty adult Indians were killed and forty were taken prisoners. Most of them sought shelter in the mountains, or behind rocks and laurel bushes for they knew this country where they had lived and hunted for many years before the white men came. If they had had arms and ammunition they would have been hard to conquer.

After the destruction of the Indian villages in Pickens County, Col. Montgomery and Capt. Grant marched their men to the Middle and Overhill villages. They destroyed fifteen Indian villages and hundreds of acres of crops, and thousands of Cherokees were driven into the Great Smokies. Only a small percentage of the white soldiers were lost but they were completely exhausted. They returned to Fort Prince George in July.

After their soldiers had rested Montgomery and Grant made another peace offer to the Cherokees. Fifteen of the head Chiefs came to Fort Prince George to discuss their proposal for peace. Attakulla-kulla was one of these. The other fourteen Chiefs, who idolized Attakulla, said they would agree to anything that he was willing to sign.

The English soldiers wrote an agreement which was translated to the Indians. Attakulla-kulla objected to one clause which stated that four Cherokee Indians should be delivered and put to death in front of them at Fort Prince George. Attakulla-kulla was firm in his refusal and asked permission to appeal to Governor Bull in Charlestown. His request was granted. Few statesmen of our present day have more will-power and good sound judgment than that old Indian Chief who once roamed the forest paths of Pickens County, South Carolina.

Governor Bull realized that Lyttleton and others had been too drastic with the Cherokees. Assuming their viewpoint, he saw in them a sacred purpose of trying to protect what they believed to be rightfully theirs. And he believed that haste and unfair treatment had brought on the Indian war.

Taking Attakulla-kulla by the hand he said:

"You were once a good friend to the English. Now that you have applied for peace let us hear what you have to say."

Attakulla-kulla asked for fire to light his pipe, and then passed it to the Governor and members of his Council. It had always been the custom of his people to smoke the peace-pipe after war. Then he brought forth a string of wampum from each of the Cherokee towns as another promise of peace.

"We live in the same land," he said. "I hope we may live in peace. Our warriors would have been less than a bunch of old women if they had not defended their homes."

Then Governor Bull told him that upon the advice of his Council they had decided to take out the clause in the agreement that Attakulla-kulla did not like. But they must cease to murder each other's men.

"We shall expect you to be faithful to the rest of the agreement," he said. "We want peace and we want our people to have homes among you and carry on the trade that we enjoyed with you before this war."

Uneducated Indian that he was Attakulla-kulla was a good speaker, and before the chiefs went back to the mountains he had bound all of them in the agreement with Governor Bull and his Council that the Cherokees would keep peace with white settlers if given fair treatment.

28

The Cherokees remained loyal to the English, according to the pledges they had made, until the Revolutionary War came on, and then they were in trouble again. It was hard for them to understand how to discriminate between the patriots and the loyalists. They had sworn to remain true to the King and they did. They fought with the Brtiish against any settlers who were not loyalists—which brought more Indian trouble to Pickens County.

Fort Prince George was not kept in good repair and was completely disbanded during the Revolutionary War. It rapidly fell into decay and all sign of it passed away except for a few cannon balls and Indian arrow heads that were found there as the years passed. The site of it has been a cultivated cornfield for at least a hundred years. The big mulberry tree that once stood beside the fort was cut down about 1925, but one of its sprouts has grown into a sizeable tree. The Fort Prince George Chapter, Daughters of the American Revolution, Pickens County, owns a gavel made from the wood of that first mulberry tree.

In 1930 the Historical Society of South Carolina placed a boulder with a bronze marker on the roadside near the original site of the fort—a small reminder of the important part Fort Prince George played in the early history of Pickens County.

Chapter Three

After Chief Attakulla agreed to the Peace Treaty of 1763 the remaining "Lower Hill" Cherokees gave no trouble in the section that is now Pickens County for about ten years. Only four or five tribes remained on the east side of Keowee River. Some had gone to join the "Overhill" or middle tribes and some were in the back, unsettled part of what is now Oconee County. "Ensenaka", a village of "Seneca Indians," who had originally drifted this way from New York State, was near the present bridge over the Seneca River at Clemson. A marker for the site of that village was placed near that bridge by the South Carolina Daughters of the American Revolution in the 1930's.

When word went out to North Carolina and Virginia that the Cherokees of the South had become more peaceable wagon trains of white settlers began moving in. For the most part they were Scotch and Irish families. There were no roads across the mountains. The wagon trains followed the flat lands and Indian Trails until they reached the fertile river valleys.

The Oolenoy and Eastatoe Valleys suited their fancy and twenty-five or thirty families settled there. A few who had settled earlier in the Saluda Valley soon joined them. Some of the pioneers brought pigs and chickens they had started raising in other states. Some brought seeds and cuttings of fruits and flowers. Some, even brought seeds they had saved from the "old country," as they liked to call their native land.

There was always a nostalgic note in their voices when they spoke of the heather covered hills of Scotland or the green grass of Ireland. And often their eyes would grow misty as they thought of loved ones they had left behind. Pioneering was a venture that tried the souls of men and women but those who lived through it became the bed-rock of our State and Nation.

Those first white settlers were "dirt farmers" in the deepest sense of the word, clearing the land and establishing homes and fields along the mountain streams. The lilt of Irish songs and laughter could be heard in the valleys and on the hillsides. The Irish made strong, courageous pioneers. They were warm hearted and fearless and nothing was too hard for them to undertake. At first they were not congenial with the still, Calvanistic ideas of the Scotch. Most of the Irish had a Catholic background, and some were Dissenters. The piety of one ran in a prescribed channel, and that of the other was not confined to party nor creed but stood ready to serve humanity whenever possible. When hard times and isolation finally molded them together it was good for all of them.

Most of the heads of families had brought Bibles. They held singings and prayer meetings, and Bible readings in their wagons, tents, and log cabins. There was usually a preacher, of a sort, in each wagon train. What he lacked in eloquence he made up for in usefulness. It was a consolation to have him there to perform marriage ceremonies and hold burial services when one died.

The first homes were crude log cabins with wide rock chimneys. Later they added lean-tos; and many years later, if the cabin was still standing after the Revolutionary War, they added more rooms and weatherboarded the house over the logs.

When the women were not helping in the fields or spinning and weaving cloth for their families they planted gardens and flowers. After a few years every yard had some crepe myrtle bushes and an Irish juniper or two. A continuation of these plants still exists in the Oolenoy Valley.

The rich fur trade that had existed between traders and Indian villages before the Indian War had changed. Fort

Prince George was now open but not so heavily garrisoned, as formerly. A man named John Stuart was in charge of it for a while and he was followed by Cameron. It was a trading post for the mountain valleys. Licensed traders came at intervals to barter with the Indians and white settlers for the skins and furs they had collected. The man at the trading post kept a supply of guns, ammunition, and a few farming tools and household necessities. Nobody bought groceries. They raised what food they had at home and gathered wild things. Providence was good to them. Fish and game were plentiful. Blackberries and plums ripened on the creek banks. In the Fall muscadines and fox grapes ripened on the hillsides and spread their fragrance through the wods. Bee trees were full of sour-wood honey, famous even then. They were glad that Fort Prince George was near, it gave them a feeling of security.

Stragglers and horse thieves were the greatest menace to the "back country" white settlers at that time. They came through pretending they were traders and ran off in the night with horses and cows they had stealthily driven into the woods. It was a great loss and inconvenience to the settlers. And some men were killed trying to recover their stolen property.

The nearest Court was in Charlestown until 1769, when Ninety-six District was formed. After that a Court House was built at Cambridge and many criminals from the "back country" were brought to justice. In less than two years thirty-two horse thieves were tried and convicted.

But peace did not last long for the pioneers. There were no newspapers, no radio nor TV, but the occasional traders brought tales of trouble that was brewing. They told of unfair taxation by the "mother country." And one of them told of the "Boston tea-party" that was causing trouble. The pioneer settlers laughed that off. Why should they bother about tea? They could go to the hillsides and get sassafras roots. They felt in need of the protection of the "mother country" in this strange new land with its native savages. Their Indian neighbors were giving no trouble, and some of them were planting fruit trees and trying to learn the farming methods of the white men, but there was always a little feeling of uneasiness.

Many South Carolinians were loyal to Britain in the beginning. But when Fort Moultrie was stormed and South Carolina blood was shed most of them were ready to fight, and when the agent at Fort Prince George began stirring up trouble with the Cherokees and offering them guns and ammunition to help England the trouble in this section really began. The Indians didn't know the difference in patriots and loyalists and one incident after another brought on trouble. The white settlers lived in terror. When the Cherokees went on the warpath at least two white families in Pickens County were massacred, and others were scalped. For generations local historians have pointed out the graves of a "Sinkler" family in the Crow Creek section, and mentioned members of Anderson, Nimmons, and Bowie families who were murdered in the Eastatoe Valley.

The Governor appointed Cpt. Andrew Williamson, a noted Indian fighter, from Abbeville to move an army of volunteers into the "back Country" before the white settlers were annihilated.

Cpt. Williamson began his invasion by routing and burning "Ensenaka" village. Fort Rutledge was built on the present Clemson College property to be used as a stockade for white settlers, while the battles were raging. Williamson and his men had an encampment on Eighteen Mile Creek.

At about the same time that white settlers had come to the Oolenoy Valley others had settled in what is now Anderson County. And volunteers from these were added to Cpt. Williamson's force. Two young men—Capt. Andrew Pickens, and Capt. Robert Anderson were among the Abbeville troops.

Some of the older histories say that Cpt. Williamson had more than 1000 men and 330 horsemen. He rode with the horsemen to attack a party of Indians and Tories and his horse was shot from under him. Some of his men were killed and some were wounded, but he escaped unharmed. The route they followed was through pathless woods and up and down very steep hills. The trees and undergrowth were almost impenetrable. It took the army five days to go twenty-five miles. They were attacked on the front and on the rear by savages who were hidden in the woods. But Cpt. Williamson with the help of Capt. Andrew Pickens and other good leaders finally put the savages to flight. Some of the prisoners they took were found to be Tories painted and disguised as Indians.

On the 13th of September 1776 Cpt. Williamson's Army was joined by a part of the North Carolina Militia and "they marched into the valley nearest the mountains." We are told that they entered a long narrow valley between two ranges of mountains. It was in our section. Could it have ʾeen Eastatoe Valley that runs long and narrow from Beasley Mountain toward Keowee River? Or was it in Oconee?

The Cherokees had gathered forces from the Middle and Overhill Tribes and formed ambuscades on all the hillsides. They made good use of the ammunition the English had granted them. They put up a stiff fight. We are told that Capt. Andrew Pickens slew many of them with his sword. The Indians finally admitted defeat and fled. Many of them went to other states.

After the Indian War practically every able-bodied white man in Pickens County fought in the Revolutionary War. Some fought at Guilford Court House in North Carolina, some went to Camden, Eutaw Springs, Musgrove's Mill, and Kettle Creek, Georgia. Many of them fought at King's Moutains and Cowpens. But many Revolutionary soldiers afterwards died in Pickens County who moved here from other states after the War. Some of them had belonged to the

Maryland, Virginia, and North Carolina Militias and fell in love with the State of South Carolina when they came here to fight. Then, after the War they moved here.

Some names of Revolutionary Soldiers buried in Pickens County are: "Aiken, Alexander, Anderson, Barton, Bowen, Blassingame, Barrett, Burdine, Bowers, Brown, Carter, Curtis, Craig, Chastain, Clayton, Chapman, Chappell, Cassell, Cantrell, Dickson, Daniel, Durham, Dean, Dorr, Duncan, Edens, Easley, Finley, Griffin, Gillespie, Gresham, Gravely, Hendricks, Hughes, Hagood, Hubbard, Hunter, Hallum, Hamilton, Hunt, Holland, Hayes, Perritt, Hester, Keith, Kirksey, Lark, Lewis, Long, Lawrence, Logan, Looper, Lynch, Lesley, Morgan, McJunkin, Mauldin, Moore, Martin, McKinney, Norton, Nimmons, McWhorter, Moser, Mosely, Mullinax, Murphy, O'Dell, O'Neal, Owensby, Oliver, Orr, Owens, Pickens, Pickel, Powers, Parrott, Parsons, Pace, Porter, Roper, Rogers, Robertson, Robinson, Rosemond, Smith, Singleton, Sloan, Stansell, Sheriff, Sutherland, Tatum, Thompson, Trotter, Turner, Winchester, Whitmire and of course there are many others.

Chapter Four

The great part taken by Gen. Andrew Pickens in the Revolutionary War and his many services in making secure the independence he had helped to achieve for upper South Carolina has often been told.

The parents of Gen. Andrew Pickens moved their family from Virginia to the Waxhaws in the Carolinas about 1752. They were living there when the Indian massacre took place at Long Canes, near Abbeville, S. C. in 1760. Some of the Calhouns were murdered, a Calhoun girl named Anna was taken prisoner by the Indians, and the rest of the family escaped to the Waxhaws.

It was there that Andrew Pickens became acquainted with his future wife Rebecca Calhoun, a relative of the noted John C. Calhoun. Later the Calhoun and Pickens families moved back to Abbeville County and Rebecca Calhoun has been described by historians as a very beautiful girl. She and Andrew Pickens were married in March 1765. We are told that the wedding was an outstanding social event where the festivities lasted for several days.

Andrew Pickens had already won a name for himself as having great power to subdue the Indians, and as time went on he became Captain, Colonel, and then one of the three Partisan Generals in the Revolutionary War. Congress presented him a sword for his bravery at the Battle of Cowpens.

General Pickens had greatly admired this mountainous section of South Carolina which he had traversed thoroughly in his battles with the Cherokees and immediately after the War he established a home which he called "Hopewell" near the Seneca River, a mile southwest of the present Clemson College near the present "Cherry's Crossing" bridge.

At the close of the Revolutionary War George Washington was anxious for a lasting peace with the Cherokee Indians and he knew that Gen. Andrew Pickens understood them. He also knew that they respected Lachlan McIntosh who had been the first English officer at Fort Prince George, and was now an American Patriot. He appointed Pickens, McIntosh, and several leading men from North Carolina, Tennessee, and Georgia to meet with a large delegation of Cherokees at Hopewell in 1785 to discuss and agree on a definite Indian Boundary line.

The Conference lasted more than a week and was attended by hundreds of Indians and many white men who camped near the designated meeting place. Nancy Ward the "Beloved Woman" from one of the Overhill tribes was especially invited. Perhaps the speech she made there was one of the first public speeches made by a woman in America. She was a sister of old Chief Attakulla who had died before that time. And her father had been an English officer stationed at Fort Loudon.

The speeches were held under a great oak tree which stood for many years and was known as the "Treaty Oak."

Chief "Old Tassel" was the main speaker for the Cherokees. General Pickens explained to him, by an interpreter, that the United States had won its war with Great Britain and had now become a Nation that was anxious to care for all of its citizens. He showed the old Chief a map of the Southern District and asked him to mark the Indian boundaries that he preferred. "We want to claim you as friends," he said, "and we will enter into a treaty that will satisfy you." The old Chief looked long and earnestly at the map.

"Speak freely and accept us as the agents of our President and friend who wants justice done to you," said Gen. Pickens.

When this was interpreted to Old Tassel he replied: "The Cherokees are the natives of this land. It is but a few

37

years since the white men found it. I belong to this land. I am willing for the white men to live here as our friends, but some have taken our land without consideration. They requested a little land and then took much. Attakulla and Occonostota are dead. The treaties they signed were not for all of us."

There were other speeches that drug on for days, and a great deal of wrangling before Old Tassel handed the Commissioners a string of Wampum to confirm his desire for peace. Then he asked that Nancy Ward might speak for them.

"I hope there will be peace," Nancy told them. "I look upon white men and red men as my brothers because I belong to both races. I have seen many wars and they are not good. I hope we may grow into one great Nation together. Let us rejoice in peace so that the chain of friendship may never be broken."

The final outcome of the Conference and Treaty was that the Indians ceded practically all of upper South Carolina, certain parts of Georgia, North Carolina, and Tennessee to the white men. It is hard to realize the scope of that great, and memorable treaty that took place on the boundary of the present Pickens County and was accomplished by the man for whom we are named.

Anna Calhoun, long a prisoner of the Indians, was returned to her family after the final settlement of that Conference.

As a private citizen Gen. Andrew Pickens took a great hand in State and National affairs. He held the first Court ever held at Abbeville Court House and his son Andrew, five years old, drew the names of the first jury. That son was the Andrew Pickens who became Governor of South Carolina 1816-1818.

Gen. Andrew Pickens was a member of the Legislature. He ran the State line between North Carolina and Tennessee.

He was elected to the United States Congress in 1794. At that time there were no railroads nor stage-coaches. He traveled on horseback, riding a white horse with a silver mounted saddle. And a Negro boy on a work horse rode behind with his luggage.

Gen. Pickens was a Christian gentleman and a staunch Presbyterian. With the help of his good neighbor and friend Gen. Robert Anderson he organized a church in 1789 which they called "Hopewell." It was built of logs on a sixteen acre tract of land donated by John Miller, the first newspaper man in upper South Carolina. Gen. Andrew Pickens, Gen. Robert Anderson, and a Mr. Dickson were chosen elders when the church was first organized. John Simpson was the first supply pastor, and Dr. Thomas Reese the first pastor and the first person buried in the churchyard. The log church was burned in a few years and the present "Stone" church was erected. Gen. Pickens gave the seats which are still in the building. He is buried in the "Old Stone" churchyard.

Many white settlers had moved to upper South Carolina after the Revolution. Some were in the neighborhood of the Stone Church which was then in what was known as Pendleton County, newly established. And a village called Pendleton had been started two miles southeast of the Stone Church. Many Charleston people seeking a more healthful climate were building plantation homes in the country around Pendleton. *CharlesTown* became Charleston in 1783.

The first census in the United States was held in 1790. The records of that census show 10,402 families living in Pendleton County, 9568 white people and 834 slaves.

Gen. Andrew Pickens and his wife Rebecca Calhoun are said to have had nine children:

I. Mary Pickens, Married John Harris.

II. Ezekial Pickens, Married first Elizabeth Bonneau; second, Eliza Barksdale.

III. Ann Pickens, Married John Simpson—moved away.

IV. Jane Pickens, Married Dr. John Miller—moved to Mississippi.

V. Margaret Pickens, Married Dr. George Bowie—moved to Alabama.

VI. Andrew Pickens, Married first Susan Wilkinson: second Mary Nelson of Virginia.

VII. Rebecca Pickens, Married William Noble, son of Maj. Alexander Noble.

VIII. Catherine Pickens, Married Dr. John Hunter—moved to Alabama.

IX. Joesph Pickens, Married Caroline Henderson—moved to Alabama.

After several years Gen. Andrew Pickens and his wife moved to their plantation home called Tamassee at the "Red House" in Oconee County where he spent the rest of his life. They are buried at the Old Stone Church.

The inscription on Gen. Pickens' tomb says:

"Gen. Andrew Pckens was born 13th of Sept. 1739, He died August 11, 1817. He was a Christian, a Patriot and a Soldier. His character and actions are incorporated with the history of his Country."

Chapter Five

In 1791 Charles Cotesworth Pinckney was Governor of South Carolina. When George Washington made his Southern tour Pinckney decided to set aside "Washington District" in his honor. The District included the present Greenville, Anderson, Pickens, and Oconee Counties

The small log court house which had been built, for a season or two, at Pendleton Village was inadequate for the larger District and too far from Greenville

The following committee was appointed to select a site for the new town and Court House: Gen. Andrew Pickens, Gen. Robert Anderson, Capt. Robert Maxwell, John Bowen, James Harrison, Major John Ford, and John Hallum.

They selected a rocky site surrounded by pines about a mile southeast of the present town of Easley. At first they named it "Rockville," because the location was so rocky. But Gen. Pickens' friends wanted it named in his honor and by an Act of the Legislature the name was changed to "Pickensville."

Pickensville was the first town built in the area of the present Pickens County. Samuel Dickson, the son of Revolutionary soldier Michael Dickson, surveyed the town and laid out the streets. Federal Street ran north and south in Pickensville and it was crossed in the center by Pinckney Street. To one side a log court house was built on a foundation of solid granite. A dungeon was dug in the rock under the jail.

Some stores and homes were built and a large frame building with an open breezeway that served as a hotel, post-office, and stagecoach stop. The old hotel stood until it burned about 1930.

Pickens Chapel was the nearest Methodist Church and Carmel was the nearest Presbyterian. We have no record of a Baptist Church there. A "Pickensville" Camp Meeting ground, that later became "Mt. Olivet" was established at the present Easley. It was usual in those day to put Camp Meeting grounds some distance away from a town. And the day of Camp Meetings did not begin until about 1820, so it was not at the beginning of Pickensville.

The land where Pickensville was built was purchased from a man named "Jack Archer" who owned many thousands of acres, including the present site of Easley which was in woods then.

The "back country" was beginning to attract attention and many people of renown came to see what they could learn of it, or to enjoy its cool breezes in the summer. Many of the men sat in homemade splint bottomed chairs in the hotel breezeway and discussed National politics, religion, and the great opportunities of this new land.

Many historic events took place at the old hotel as the years passed. Banquets and balls for political occasions, and Muster meetings, and many years later the noted participants of a duel, Perry and Bynum, spent the night there before they went to Hatton's Ford where Bynum was killed.

Stagecoaches came from Augusta once a week to bring mail and passengers. It was a great event when the stagecoach driver could be heard blowing his horn down the road a piece.

Charles Pinckney and his wife had a summer home there, and many other prominent citizens lived there for a few years. Chancellor Waddy Thompson, Sr., settled first in Pickensville when he came to South Carolina from Virginia. And his son, Waddy Thompson, Jr., who had a notable political career, was born there. The Thompsons moved to Greenville after a few years.

42

Dr. John Robinson who married Eliza Blassingame (daughter of Gen. John Blassingame of Revolutionary fame), was the first doctor in Pickensville. He has descendants in Easley.

The first Court was held in the new Court House in the fall of 1792. The legal bodies planned to hold court twice a year, in the spring and fall. Washington District became a Congressional District in 1794, and that was when Gen. Andrew Pickens was elected to Congress. There were many political meetings and public speakings that were attended by men from every part of the District, which was still sparsely settled. Pendleton was on its way to becoming a nice village, but Pickensville remained the leading town until 1798 when Greenville took growing pains and decided to build its own Court House.

That was the end of Washington District, and by 1800 Pendleton District was established and included the present counties of Anderson, Pickens, and Oconee with a Court House and jail that were built on the public square at Pendleton. Then all crimes and misdemeanors of this area were tried at Pendleton for the next twenty-five years.

The removal of the Court House from Pickensville naturally stopped its growth. Some of its citizens moved to Greenville and some to Pendleton. We are told that most of the records from Washington District went to the Greenville Court House. But the village remained a village, with a post office and stage-coach stop for many years.

Mrs. Charles Pinckney, Mrs. Waddy Thompson, Sr., and others who had been reared in Virginia or Charleston, S. C., brought an atmosphere of culture to the village of Pickensville that might have seemed strange to backwoods pioneers, if they had not entertained the people with such ease and grace that no one felt awkward or left out. When they opened their small but beautifully appointed homes for an afternoon tea it lent glamour to the small village. And the ladies of the surrounding farms treasured an invitation. It was part of a girl's education to observe the grace and dignity of these women.

At first there were no schools in the village young children were taught in the homes. A boarding school for young ladies had opened at Pendleton, which was well attended by the daughters of those who were financially able to send them. And a man named Edwin Reese opened a school for young men near Pendleton.

There was very little social life between the boys and girls of the teen-age group in that time. Even buggy riding was frowned upon for a long time. But somehow courting was done and the girls married young, except a few who remained spinsters, and they usually had a sad story to tell about a lover who had died. A few traveled the primrose path as in every generation.

The local merchants always kept a few bolts of flowered challis, and sprigged muslin in colors that would tempt blue-eyed or brown-eyed girls. Most of the girls sewed very well and they learned to make the empire dresses that were stylish at that time. Sometimes young ladies came from Charleston or Augusta on the stage-coach to visit relatives in Pickensville or Pendleton, or the town called "Andersonville," a few miles southwest of Pendleton. (That was several years before the town "Anderson" had started.) Some of these ladies were wearing "poke" bonnets and empire dresses, and the style was set. Hair was curled and usually one curl was straying out across the neck line. The girls who were artistic learned to design and create remarkable reproductions of the dresses and bonnets they admired.

People who lived in the present Pickens County area had a few country stores, but two or three times a year they went to Pickensville or Pendleton to do some real shopping. And there was another store called "McBeth's" across the Saluda River on the "Island Ford" road from Greenville to Pickensville.

We do not have a complete list of merchandise carried by McBath's early store but it must have been varied and interesting. Some of the old records state that they had Bibles, household furniture, candlesticks, punch bowls, dress material, harness, and staples. Other items mentioned were gun powder, nails, tallow, and whiskey.

The farms were productive and produce was hauled by wagons to Augusta or to the nearest boat landings on the Savannah River where there were always buyers for export trade. Hamburg had not been built then. The red clay soil of Pickens County uplands was adapted to cotton growing but the practice of pulling the fiber from the seed by hand was a slow process. In 1793 when Eli Whitney invented the cotton gin it made cotton one of the great agricultural products of the United States and settlers flocked to the up-country from the coastal regions. Wagons of families often went through Pickensville on their way to Georgia and Alabama where there was more good cotton land. Land was cheap and easy to get.

If the would-be farmers held grants for War Service they could almost take their pick of land. Or they could buy it for a very small price per acre from the speculators who had acquired large holdings of land soon after the Treaty of 1785 with the Cherokees. The Bank of Charleston and the Bank of Philadelphia once owned thousands of acres in the upper part of the present Pickens County. Some of which was afterwards bought by the Carolina Timber Company and in (1958) belongs to the Poinsett Lumber & Manufacturing Company, and private citizens.

There were several early churches in the Pickens County, area between Keowee and Saluda Rivrs, even back to the foot of the mountains, and there was always a settlement around them. The people in those settlements led simple hard working lives and only a few of them felt they could afford the luxury of owning slaves. (The churches that existed at that time will be listed later).

45

In 1812 the second war with England came on. But many National things of importance had taken place before that. In 1797 John Adams was elected President of the United States, following George Washington who died in 1799 at the age of 68. In 1800 the seat of government was moved from Philadelphia to Washington. In 1798 about 4000 people died in Philadelphia in an epidemic of yellow fever, which came at intervals in all of the big cities with disastrous results, for many years.

In 1801 Thomas Jefferson and Aaron Burr tied in an election for President of the United States. In the settlement Jefferson became President and Burr Vice-president. In 1803 Jefferson made the Louisiana Purchase from the French government for fifteen million dollars, adding a great amount of unopened land to our Nation, and giving the people a great deal to talk about.

There were no radioes nor TV, no newspapers nor telephones in Pickensville. The citizens eagerly waited for the stage-coach to get the latest news. And then it quickly passed from lip to lip through the village. And it was dramatically discussed at the hotel.

There was consternation in 1804 when Aaron Burr killed Alexander Hamilton in a duel. And again in 1807 when Burr was tried for treason. Someone had received a New York newspaper through the mail, and after the citizens had scanned it eagerly they sent it over to Pendleton so that John Miller who had just started a small newspaper called "Miller's Weekly Messenger" might copy some of the items for his readers.

The War of 1812 came on because England and France were at war with each other and the American merchants were shipping goods to both. Americans had prospered unbelievably and their ships were often attacked on the high seas. Finally it became unbearable, and when British seamen began deserting their ships and coming to work for Americans for higher wages the British blockaded their ports against our ships, and the war was on.

It was an unorganized war that lasted two or three years without many battles on land. When Andrew Jackson gathered an army of backwoodsmen and won a great victory over the British at New Orleans the Americans were proud and happy.

Several men from Pickens County fought in the War of 1812. We find their tombs in various cemeteries. Dr. John Robinson was a surgeon in the War of 1812. A blacksmith named John Mauldin who lived in the George's Creek community made swords for the army; and a gun factory was established by Samuel Earle at the village called "Andersonville" below Pendleton at the head of the Savannah River. (This village is a dead town now and it had no connection with the Georgia prison town called "Andersonville.")

In 1817 the vacant Court House and several stores at Pickensville burned. After the fire an unusual circumstance took place. The people of Pendleton got up a lottery to try to raise $10,000 Pickensville Benefit.

The following is a copy of the lottery ticket: "Charitable Relief Lottery. By authority of the State of South Carolina No. 4869. This ticket will entitle the holder to such prize as may be drawn against this number, in a lottery to be drawn at Pendleton Court House, S. C., for the relief of sufferers by fire at Pickensville, S. C. If demanded within twelve months after the drawing is completed. James C. Griffin, Manager, Pendleton, S. C."

This lottery ticket appeared in the March 31, 1818 "Pendleton Messenger," and in the Statutes of South Carolina.

Millers Weekly Messenger had developed into a larger newspaper and was published for many years as "The Pendleton Messenger." It was the first newspaper in upper South Carolina and for many years the only one. From 1809 until

1850 it gave political, legal, and some social news, land transfers and advertisements, and produce prices. And whatever news the editors could gather from a distance. They prided themselves on foreign news.

Some items taken from the newspaper to show names of local people living in the Pickens County area. Feb. 28, 1818:

"We are authorzed to state that Samuel H. Dickson, of Pickensville is a candidate for the Senate of South Carolina."

"Dr. William Anderson is a candidate for the honor of representative of Pendleton District in the State Legislature."

"Land sales: 100 acres of land, more or less, on the waters of Twelve Mile. Property of Joseph Patterson."

"Two hundred acres on Cane Creek, James McGuffin."

"Wolf Creek: Dissolution of store partnership of James Hunter and Lemul Gustin. March 8, 1818."

Managers of election at Dr. William Brown's store, Aug. 5, 1818: "Bailey Barton, Henry Cobb, Nathan Boon, James McKinney, Jeptha Norton, Daniel Liddell."

Political: "Sept. 5, 1820—We are authorized to announce that Col. Benjamin Hagood is a candidate for the State Legislature from the Twelve Mile section of Pendleton District." (Mr. Hagood was elected and another newspaper of a later date says that he was influential in getting a certain bridge built over Eighteen Mile Creek, and the bridge was called "Hagood's Bridge."

After Washington District had ceased and the Court House had been moved back to Pendleton the "Farmer's Society" was organized in 1815.

In 1820 Robert Mills, the famous architect and statistitian published "Mill's Atlas of Pendleton District, South Carolina." In the part of the map that is now Pickens County he listed all of our familiar creeks and rivers and mountains just as we know them in 1958. But the only towns in the area were Pickensville and Pumpkintown, both plainly marked.

Chapter Six

In 1826 Pendleton District was divided into Anderson and Pickens Districts. They were named respectively for Gen. Robert Anderson, and Gen. Andrew Pickens. Pickens District included the present Oconee and Pickens Counties. This change was approved by an Act of the Legislature December 20, 1826.

The Commissioners appointed to run the dividing line were: "Col. J. C. Kilpatrick, Major Lewis, and Thomas Garvin."

The Commissioners to select a site for a town and Court House were: "J. C. Kilpatrick, Andrew Hamilton, R. H. Briggs, William Beavert, and Jabez Jones. They were authorized to buy a tract of land from one hundred to four hundred acres. It must be located near the center of Pickens District.

The Commissioners appointed to have the public buildings erected were: "G. W. Liddell, Tarlton Lewis, Nathan Boone, Thomas B. Reed, and James McKinney, Sr."

The various groups of Commissioners proceeded with their duties and made their resports to the next session of the General Assembly which passed an Act of approval December 19, 1827. This Act was to go into effect from the second Monday of October 1828, on which date the division became effective and Anderson and Pickens became separate Judicial Districts. But Pickens did not become an election district until 1854.

The buildings had been erected as specified, a frame Court House, which stood for forty years.

The first court was held in the Court House at Old Pickens in October 1828. Maj. William L. Keith was elected the first Clerk of Court. He served until 1856, when he was succeeded by James E. Hagood who served until 1868 when Pickens District was divided into the present Oconee and Pickens Counties.

A traditional story has often been told of the way the Commissioners selected the location for the town which they named "Pickens" (now a dead town spoken of as "Old Pickens').

There were only a few wagon roads then and bridle paths through the woods. The Commissioners rode horseback over the central part of the District. They stopped on a high hill beside the Keowee River to eat their basket lunch. Someone remarked about the beauty of the mountains from that hilltop, and then they talked of the clear running stream, with its possibilities for water power. They decided then and there that this was the ideal place for a town, and before they started home they drove a stake in the ground to designate the place for the new Court House.

The families who helped to make "Old Pickens" a flourishing town for forty years were: Alexander, Kirksey, Craig, Robins, Norton, Adams, Gresham, Calhoun, Kennemur, McKinney, Nimmons, Anderson, Harris, Parrott, Hunnicut, Ramsey, Hughes, Powers, Seaborn, Kay, Curtis, Hagood, Capehart, Lay, Burgess, Foster, Barton, Hunter, Boone, Carter, Mauldin, Glenn, Hamilton, Thompson, Keith, Finley, Stewart, Knox, Doyle, Davis, Rogers, Wilson, McFall, Langston, Hunt, Gibson, Hendricks, Johnson, Whitmire, Gaines, Breazeale, Brown, Steele, Moss, Reed, Liddell, Lee, and many others.

The houses that were built would be a credit to our modern times. They were not luxurious but substantial and homelike, for most of the citizens were people of culture and refinement. Only one of the houses has been kept in good repair, the Pleasant Alexander home. It is in plain view of the present river bridge, up the stream a few hundred yards. It passed out of the family many years ago and in 1958 belongs to the Hill family. Another beautiful home was a brick house now falling into decay on the Pickens-Walhalla highway. It was the Miles Norton home. There was a hotel and a schoolhouse on the hill near the Court House.

In 1830 a brick church with a slave gallery was built on the first hill above the river. Soon there was a cemetery around it. The church was Presbyterian in the beginning. After Old Pickens became a dead town it was taken over for a while by the Methodist Mission Board, but it later changed to Presbyterian again.

Mr. Sam McFall and Mr. Silas Kirksey each had a turn at running the hotel, and a Mr. Morgan is also mentioned. Mr. Kirksey was the first Post Master, and then Mr. Pleasant Alexander served as Post Master for many years. There was a stage-coach line from Greenville to Dahlonega, Georgia that brought mail and passengers to Old Pickens twice a week. The stage drove four horses and changed horses every fifteen miles. One stage-coach stop where they changed horses was near the old Prater Schoolhouse (1958). The country Post Offices sent men on horseback to the stage-stop to pick up their mail.

There were no river bridges in that day. Ferries crossed the river at intervals and there were many fords. Robertson's Ford was just blow the present river bridge at Old Pickens.

A great deal of business was carried on by boat traffic down the Keowee and Seneca Rivers to the head of the Savannah River at Andersonville where bigger boats came from Augusta and Savannah to gather loads of country produce. A boat channel was kept cleared at one side of the streams. There was much talk of a new town called "Hamburg" on the South Carolina side of Augusta.

Some of the plantation owners lived in the town of Old Pickens and practiced law or other professions and their slaves tended the fertile Keowee valleys in corn and cotton and tobacco to be sent to market in boats.

51

As the years passed there were big social functions and weddings where the entertainment lasted for several days and guests came from Charleston, Augusta, and Abbeville. Beautiful wedding gowns were often made in Charleston for these occasions. We have heard of one made of white satin with a filmy lace overskirt.

The sons and daughters of the people who had wealth were sent away from home to complete their education and some of them fell in love while they were attending school in other towns. Others married the boys and girls they had always known and settled in the community.

But life has its joys and sorrows whether we live in a quiet, dreamy place or in a bustling city. One of the young Alexander girls, who was an excellent horsewoman, was out riding one day when the horse became frightened and ran away with her. She was thrown against a tree and killed. It cast a gloom over Old Pickens for weeks. She was buried in the Old Pickens churchyard.

In 1828 when Pickens District was formed the local road building was carried on by Commissioners of roads who were appointed by the General Assembly. Those appointed for Pickens District were: William G. Field, Joseph Evatt, Jeptha Norton, Jr., Frederick N. Garvin, Stephen C. Reed, Weyman Holland, and John Hunter. These men met and selected their own chairman. They were also allowed to elect a clerk and treasurer, who must give bond with securities approved by the Board. All able-bodied men were liable to both road duty and militia duty.

The Commissioners were appointed for a term of three years. From time to time they were asked to repair or locate roads (dirt roads through the woods). A certain amount of tax money went for this purpose and they were asked to collect fees from new tavern keepers or retailers of spirituous liquors; to sign and issue all warrants and executions of the Board, and to receive the money collected from fines, licenses, and the sale of extras. All records were supposed to be kept in order for public inspection.

Men were trained for Militia duty at Muster Grounds scattered over the District. In case of war they would not be totally unprepared.

There was no Department of Public Welfare then but Commissioners of the Poor were appointed for a two year term of office and they were fined if they failed to serve. They were authorized to erect an almshouse in the District—and to inspect the living conditions of widows, orphans, and paupers throughuot the District. If funds were available they would help to educate bright, deserving children of the poor. The almshouse for Pickens District was run by Mr. Daniel Hughes who lived on the Pickens County side of Keowee River.

Some of the other County officers of Pickens District were: "Sheriff: S. Reed 1829-1840; F. N. Garvin 1840-44; P. Alexander 1844-48; J. A. Doyle 1848-52; Alexander Bryce 1852-56; L. C. Craig 1856-60; Wm. N. Craig 1860-64; Lemuel Thomas 1864-68.

Clerk of Court: W. L. Keith 1829-56; J. E. Hagood 1856-68.

W. L. Keith, the first Clerk of Court, had two sons who became prominent lawyers. The elder, Col. Elliot Keith, was a talented speaker. In 1849 he founded the newspaper, "The Keowee Courier" at Old Pickens. The motto was: "To thine ownself be true, and it must fellow as the night the day; thou can'st not then be false to any man." He remained the editor of the paper for four years until he was called into Service in the Civil War. The paper suspended publication for a while during the War, and then started again under Trimmer and Thompson until it moved to Walhalla when Pickens District was divided.

Calhoun Keith started practicing law in Old Pickens and later moved to Walhalla. Another lawyer who began practice at Old Pickens and moved to Walhalla was Joseph

J. Norton. He came to the Bar in 1856 and stayed until 1861, when he and his father Miles M. Norton responded to the call for volunteers and organized Company C and E of Orr's Regiment of Rifles. Miles M. Norton was killed at the Second Battle of Manasses in 1862. Col. Joseph Norton was disabled and came home and took charge of the Enlistment Bureau.

The 1830's, 40's, and 50's were eventful years at Old Pickens. Andrew Jackson was President of the United States and the Vice-President, John C. Calhoun, had recently moved to his home "Fort Hill" near Pendleton. Calhoun resigned from the Vice-Presidency when he grew bitter over the question of State's Rights and Nullification.

Many South Carolinians were on his side but some were against him. Some believed that Jackson was a plain man, a friend of the people. Let him run things. They were more inclined to worry about the abolition movement that had started in the North.

Spurred on by the abolitionists some slaves in Virginia had recently murdered a number of white people. And slave owners were greatly concerned over that.

The Cherokee Indians in Georgia started giving trouble about that time. They did not want to abide by Georgia's laws. But President Jackson sympathized with the Georgians. He made the Cherokees a proposition to surrender their lands in Georgia, Alabama, and Mississippi to the white men and accept five million dollars and some land west of the Mississippi River.

The deal was made and the Georgia Cherokees, and many of those in the back corner of South Carolina went west. A sad procession.

Then the Seminole War in Florida came on. A few men from Anderson and Pickens Districts went to fight in that war, as old records of soldiers, and old gravestones tell us.

Martin Van Buren was elected President of the United States in 1837 and was obliged to face the worst depression that American had known in a long time. It had come by Jackson's policy of putting all Government money in State Banks, and allowing an orgy of speculating that was done by exchanging notes through the banks. Soon the banks could not extend credit, and even the Government could not meets its obligations.

Many citizens of Pickens District went west, seeking escape from present troubles, and new opportunities. Mormon Missionaries came through Anderson and Pickens Districts and got some converts for their church.

In the late 1840's the California gold rush created a new incentive to move west, and several families joined wagon trains that were passing through. Stephen Foster's music was popular then. The young people were singing "Jeanie With the Light Brown Hair," and every Negro was picking "Sussanah Don't You Cry For Me" on his banjo.

That was about the time that George Cook a photographer and daguerrotype artist in Charleston was training artists and sending them into the "back country" to make tin-types and daguerrotypes. It proved to be remunerative business, for before that time no one had pictures of their loved ones unless someone painted them, and the expense of that was prohibitive. And artists were scarce.

A great many tin-types and daguerrotypes made at Old Pickens more than a hundred years ago are in homes in Pickens County today.

A record book still exists of School Commissioners of Pickens District from 1837 to 1852. The names of these men were: Joseph Gresham, Chairman; Wm. L. Keith, Secretary and Treasurer; Silas Kirksey, Joseph B. Reid, F. N. Garvin, Samuel Mosely, J. R. Cox, W. C. Lee, J. A. Doyle, J. L. Kennedy, and M. Jones. The same officers served from 1828 to 1852.

The records had been carefully kept in the fine handwriting of W. L. Keith. At the first meeting the Commissioners fixed the salaries of teachers, as follows: $10 per annum per child for first class teachers—$8 per annum for second class teachers; $6 per annum for third class teachers. These salaries were for teaching the free pupils who were limited in number to four, six, or eight for each school, and this was paid by the District. Parents who were financially able had to pay tuition for their children. In 1837 the whole of Pickens District had twenty-two schools, eleven in what is now Pickens County and eleven on the west side of the Keowee River.

The prospective teachers were examined by the Commissioners and graded according to their ability. The best qualified always taught the more advanced students. The Academy in Old Pickens had the best teachers they could afford, for most of the students in town were able to pay tuition. Old Pickens was incorporated as the town of Pickens in 1847 with a population of more than 1600.

Pickens District was proud of its Court House town and all legal business and transfers of property from the Georgia line to the Saluda River were handled there. And all criminals received punishment there.

An element of superstition had lingered in the best of families from their Welsh and Irish ancestors, and the Negro farm hands and servants in the community were extremely superstitious. A traditional story is told of a double hanging on the Court House hill at Old Pickens that almost threw the whole population into a panic.

The summer day was bright and clear when the crowd began to gather that morning for the serious and solemn occasion. Men came on horseback and in wagons and buggies. No lady would venture farther than her front door at such a time, but their curiosity was aroused to the point of gazing out the windows at the gathering crowd, keeping the children inside, and making sure that enough dinner was being cooked to take care of extra guests. And suddenly before mid-morning they noticed that the sunlight had a weird, unholy look. It gave them an uncanny feeling.

And over on the hilltop the men had noticed it, too. The scaffold had been built, the black caps were ready, the Sheriff had just been out to see that everything was in readiness, and a preacher had gone in to have a last prayer with the murderers.

There wasn't a cloud in the sky but the atmosphere was murky. The men began to gather in little groups and talk about it. Queerest thing they'd ever seen. Maybe the Lord wasn't willing they should hang men. Not two at one time, anyway.

The little procession came out of the jail with the first man. The black cap was adjusted, he went on the scaffold and dropped. It was soon over. The preacher murmured a prayer, and the sky was getting darker by the minute. Mules were beginning to bray over in the hitching yard and dogs were beginning to howl. Men began slipping away and the rattle of wagons was soon heard on the curve of the rocky road beyond the river.

By the time the last criminal had mounted the scaffold and dropped only a few of the town's citizens remained; and although it was early noon the sky was as dark as midnight. Some of the old Negroes were on their knees praying and some of the younger ones were stretched on the ground.

The Clerk of Court came out of the Court House and started toward his home to dinner. Most of the homes had been named, his was "Jasmine Cottage." As he went along the path in the dark he stumbled over one of his servants lying prostrate.

The Negro boy jumped up. "Why it's you, Pete," said his master. "This darkness won't hurt you. The almanac said this was the day for a total eclipse of the sun. I should have warned you boys." He was trying to be very casual.

"Yas suh," said Pete, his teeth still chattering. He evidently could not understand it. But he believed his master.

"It's something we don't have more than once in a lifetime," the man explained, "when the moon comes between the earth and the sun for a little while. You see, it's beginning to get light again already." And he started up the path with Pete following.

Weather conditions often hindered the river traffic of the early settlers. Floods sometimes damaged the mills that were run by water power, sometimes even washed them away.

The winter of 1835 was the coldest winter reported in the Nation until that time. All of the mountain streams were frozen, and it was impossible for boats to travel the Savannah River. The summer of 1845 was so dry that all of the smaller streams dried up and the fish died. The larger streams only had a small trickle of water down the center and were unfit for boat travel. (Traditional story handed down by mountain families).

But in 1847 there came the worst floods they had ever experienced. Water rose thirty-seven feet above any known water marks, and this is true because the river town of Andersonville, at the headwaters of the Savannah River, was practically washed away and was never rebuilt.

Chapter Seven

While Old Pickens on Keowee River was a thriving town the present area of Pickens County was not asleep, between 1826 and 1860.

It was not thickly settled and there were no good roads, but there were many good home and churches and many Postoffices in homes or country stores. Some of the Postoffices were: "Meet, Five Mile, Salubrity, Praters, Hunters, Browns, Dalton, Crete, Nimmons, Murphy, Antioch, Crow Creek, Eastatoe, Stewarts, Oolenoy, Mayfields, Gravely, Ambler, Pumpkintown, Rock, Flower, Knob, Briggs, Cross Roads, Hunts, Pickensville, and others. A man on horseback took the mail from the stagecoach stop to a certain number of Postoffices.

The citizens went to "Pickens Court House," as they called it, to shop or to attend to business. Sometimes they went to Greenville, which had grown into a nice village by that time. The young people went to the schools nearest them, sometimes a distance of four or five miles. When they grew older a few of them went to school at Pickens C. H., or Pickensville, or maybe to Pendleton, if their families were financially able to send them.

There were many homes and farms along Keowee River, for the fertile valleys produced wonderful crops and Hendricks, Alexander, Craigs, Steele's, McKinney's, Robertsons, Reed and Lawrences had been granted land as early settlers. Others who owned homes on the Pickens County side were Ramseys, Powers, Hughes, Kings, Whitmires and Bookers. The Careys, Curtis, Kirkseys and others who lived on the west side of Keowee later moved to Pickens County.

The last house on the Pickens County side of the river in the 1840s was the mansion home of John Ewing Calhoun, a brother of Mrs. John C. Calhoun, who had married her cousin. The home was named "Keowee Heights." It stood on a hill overlooking the place where Twelve Mile and Keowee come together, forming Seneca River. It was one of the finest of the old homes built in the up-country, a large white frame house with big columns and a circular portico. There is no photograph available for it burned before the Civil War. Old letters and papers describe it as looking like fairyland in the spring when hundreds of white dogwood trees bloomed in the surrounding forest and the river banks were covered with blooming laurel.

The Calhouns were from Charleston. They had come to the up-country on account of unhealthful conditions on the coast. They had a number of slaves and did a great deal of entertaining. One of their sons was killed in a duel with a Rhett man from Charleston and lies buried in the family graveyard which was near the house.

They had a small cloth-making plant on the place, and a tan-yard for making boots and shoes for the slaves. They also had a large grist mill for grinding born corn and wheat. After Mr. Calhoun died one thing advertised at his sale was "a pair of French Burr mill stones, of great size and depth."

The late Miss Olive Boggs Newton of Pickens had some chairs that came from the John E. Calhoun home.

Sheriff Doyle of Pickens District bought the place after the Calhouns died but it burned before the Civil War and was never rebuilt.

Mrs. John E. Calhoun, Sr., mother of Mrs. John C. and John E. Calhoun Jr. also had a fine home which was described in A Pendleton Messenger as being "A very fine type of Colonial home." It was named "Cold Springs' and stood near the present Clemson-Calhoun Elementary School, just up the road a short distance from Keowee Heights. John E. Calhoun, Sr. was one of the first U. S. Senators from Charleston District and this was their summer home. It was also in Pickens

County. These homes were built early in 1800. Mr. Aaron Boggs was John C. Calhoun's plantation overseer. His old home is near the Newton Lumber place. 1958.

Wherever churches had been established there were several comfortable homes in the community. And a grist mill on almost every big farm.

The Calhouns attended the old St. Paul's Episcopal Church at Pendleton. Carmel and the Old Stone Church were the nearest Presbyterian churches. There were several homes around Carmel of more than average prominence. The Hallum, Hamilton, Walker, Boggs, Templeton, and others.

A traditional story has alawys been told about the beginning of a church at Liberty (Baptist Church). This is the story: "The Baptist people of the community were holding a meeting at their little log church near "Salubrity Spring, and the Salubrity post office, which was in the home of a Mr. Bill Williams.

When the news came that peace had been declared between the United States and Great Britain the congregation shouted that their church should henceforth be called "Liberty" church."

Old church records in the Clemson College Library state: "The early origin of Liberty Church in Pickens County is slight. It claims 1780, most likely between 1780-1790. It entered Saluda Baptist Association in 1817." This church is not to be confused with another Liberty Baptist Church near Westminster, which was also in Pickens District, but not in the present Pickens County. 1840 the Rev. Bryan Boroughs was justice of the peace at Pickensville. He superintended the building of the present brick church at old Carmel.

Secona Baptist Church near the present town of Pickens was organized 1786-1789; Liberty 1780-1790; Oolenoy 1789; Keowee 1791; Cross Roads 1795; Antioch (early, date not given); Peter's Creek (early, date not given. These are the churches reported at the organizational meeting of the

61

"Twelve Mile River Baptist Association" at Secona Church in 1829. (Note: Griffin Baptist Church did not join the Twelve Mile Association until 1857, but there is a tradition that it is about the age of Cross Roads. The Baptist Missionary, Elnathan Davis is believed to have founded it because he is buried there and he died in 1821.) It was not named "Griffin" until 1856 when Sargeant Griffin gave the land for "Griffin Church."

This record is given of Keowee Baptist Church: "This church was organized in 1791. It entered Bethel Association in 1793. The Rev. Joseph Logan became pastor between 1791-1796 with seventeen members. The church was built on a two acre lot, originally granted to Joseph Gresham near Fort Prince George. The church entered Saluda Association 1802, and Twelve Mile Association 1829." Steeles, Craigs, Hendricks, Mauldins, Robins, Alexanders, Boones, Nimmons and Murphys were among its early members. There were comfortable and well kept log homes in the community surrounding the church.

In that period between 1826 and 1860 other Baptist churches reported to the Twelve Mile Association were: "Newhope, 1832, Benjamin Head Supply, 44 members; Six Mile 1836 Mt. Carmel, Dacusville, added to the second Union Meeting District 1837 (Organized earlier). Holly Springs (first called Bethlehem) 1847, M. Chastain Supply, 35 members; Mountain Grove 1850, M. Chastain, 19 members. Enon 1850, W. B. Singleton, 19 members. (new brick church built in 1854.) Fairview, 1858, F. Findley, 15 members; George's Creek 1859, L. Von Supply, 13 members. (May have been organized earlier).

Very early Methodist churches were: Bethlehem, near present town of Pickens. First called "Tatum Church," changed to Bethlehem. Dacusville Methodist Church first called the trap and Antioch Methodist Church are known to be the outgrowth of sermons preached by Bishop Francis Asbury as he passed through this section riding horseback from Philadelphia to Charleston, S. C. to attend the Methodist Conference about 1789. Other very old Methodist churches are: Tabor, between Pickens and Easley organized 1842 (or earlier). Zion, below Easley. Ruhama, near Liberty; Fairview, near Central, and Gap Hill in the western part of Pickens County. Glassy Mountain, Methodist, discontinued in the 1890s was said to be an Asbury church.

Many churches have not kept written records which makes it difficult to state the exact date they were organized.

Camp-meetings originated in Kentucky about 1800 and spread into the Carolinas. They were more or less union meetings of the several denominations providing their best preachers. They usually had a large arbor for open air meetings and tents for the people from a distance who came and camped while the meetings lasted for several days. The Twelve Mile Camp Ground was about three miles west of Pickens, on the present Pickens-Walhalla highway. It had a large arbor for camp meetings and a small church for year round purposes. It stood there through the eighties and nineties, after the town of Pickens had been here for several years. The Rev. W. C. Seaborn, a Baptist pastor, was one of the visiting preachers at the Methodist Twelve Mile Camp Ground. He lived in the Prater's Creek community of Pickens County and had been appointed Moderator for the Twelve Mile River Baptist Association. His father Henning Frederick Seaborn was a native of Germany and had been reared a Lutheran. W. C. Seaborn was born and reared in a German settlement in Oconee County and had moved to Pickens County. His sermons were admired for their strength, and *length,* if you liked long sermons.

An item in a Pickens Sentinel in the late 1880's said: "W. C. Seaborn preached at the Twelve Mile Camp Ground Sunday and held his hearers spellbound for two hours and twenty minutes."

Oolenoy Church had a large membership of early white settlers that spread over the Oolenoy Valley. It was near Pumpkintown and near Table Rock. It had a store and Postoffice and a Sutherland and Keith boarding house very early. In 1848 Mr. Keith built a hotel near the mountain. Table Rock was famous then for its scenic beauty and a big celebration was held there for the opening of the hotel which was attended by the governors of both North and South Carolina. A cannon was to be dragged to the top of the mountain and fired but a driving rain hindered that part of the celebration. Col. J. E. Hagood who later became one of the founders of Pickens attended the celebration.

A man from a distant state visited Table Rock in 1842. His trip was written up in "Orion Magazine 1842," a part of the article follows:

"Table Rock is five miles distant from Pumpkintown and we were informed that we should have to pass over a new causeway constructed expressly for the passage of carriages to the base of the Rock. The road, though tolerable, is not one that tourists would enjoy. There is a toll-gate with a fee of seventy-five cents. This turn-pike runs along the top of the base from which the mountain rises so that for a time the traveler loses the magnificent view of the Rock perched on its throne. But there is a foot route through the valley where one never loses the view. We decided on the foot route.

"A right angled descent in our path revealed one of the most charming views we have ever encountered. In the foreground lay the pastoral beauty of the cove with its greensward and some cultivated fields, and a most picturesque log cabin. In the distance was a line of mountains, and facing us was the mighty Rock

"After making many sketches we passed the night in the log cabin and the second morning took a toilsome ramble to the foot of the Rock on the eastern facade. We passed a small lake, properly called "the pool." It was filled with pieces of rock that had fallen from the mountain.

"Someone at an earlier day had bolted wooden steps to the face of the Rock. We counted 130 steps. They are substantially built, with a hand rail or bannister, which made the passage safe and tolerably easy.

"From the summit we enjoyed a wide, enchanting panorama. The top of the Rock is comparatively level. In many places the surface is stony, in other alluvial and covered with noble trees. Near the center we found the remains of a hut which we were told had been planned as the kitchen of a proposed hotel. Though the enterprise was given up it could be possible. There are fifty or sixty acres of tenable land, and a spring of purest water and coolness."

Another mountain called "Caesar's Head," just over the line in Greenville County, was always popular and well known to the people of Pickens County because it belonged to Col. Benjamin Hagood, a native of this section. He owned many thousands of acres in the upper part of Pickens County. His home and the family graveyard where he is buried are in the Twelve Mile section of Pickens County. One summer along in the 1840's he decided to build a cottage on Caesar's Head and take his family there to enjoy the beautiful views and the cooling breezes. They had visitors who urged him to make it a summer resort and he did that. He moved to Caesar's Head but his sons continued to live in Pickens County. His eldest son John lived at the home place in this county for several years, but finally moved to Greenville County to the old Goodwin place. James E. Hagood built a home near the family graveyard and left it to move to "Old Pickens." The Hagood Grist Mill and store continued to operate through the years.

The first Ambler home was a big two - story house that still stands across the highway from the Fred Findley home (1958). Ambler Postoffice and a barter store operated there very early. A man named Ben Noble directed it and hauled produce to Hamburg (later North Augusta). The James Ambler who built this house was a graduate of William and Mary College in Virginia. He came to Edgefield, S. C. to teach school and married Susan Hagood, a member of the Edgefield family of Hagoods. On account of the more healthful climate they came to Pickens District to live. Their son, James Hagood Ambler, built the other Ambler home farther up the road toward Pumpkintown, near the present Ambler School. He married Miss Zealy Cox of Greenville.

The Boldings and Garretts were early settlers in the Pea Ridge section of Pickens County which is near Six Mile. Prater's Creek Postoffice and store was located at the Boroughs home and Grist Mill on Prater's Creek. The farm and mill remained in the Boroughs family for about seventy-five years. One of the daughters, Miss Jane Boroughs, was a well loved Sunday school teacher in the community for about forty years.

Hunter's Store, Postoffice, Home and Muster Ground were located a few miles west of the present town of Pickens. A Pendleton Messenger of 1837 tells of a July 4th celebration held there. We quote:

"The celebration was carried off in fine style. About 300 citizens partook of barbecued beef, lamb, chickens, home cooked bread, pies, and cakes.

"The Rev. McGuffin opened the program with prayer. An Artillery Company was present and toasts were drunk at the firing of the cannon. Then the Declaration of Independence was read by Prof. Edwin Reese. This was followed by a patriotic speech by C. P. Dupree."

Politics ran high, even in those days, between contending parties. Each country store had its political rally and speaking date to which all of the surrounding community came. Waddy Thompson, Jr. who was born at Pickensville, S. C. was running for Congress in the 1840's as a whig candidate. He was a noted speaker with a glowing personality. The Democrats were fearful he would be elected and planned several big barbecues where they arranged for John C. Calhoun to speak for their candidate, Mr. Earle, who was a fine man but not a good speaker.

And neither was Calhoun a good stump speaker. His dignified personality and scholarly remarks were better suited for senatorial halls. The rural people understood little about the sub-treasury and other dry technical subjects that Calhoun dwelt on.

On the other hand Thompson's speeches were full of rollicking anecdotes. Following one of Calhoun's sub-treasury talks he told this story:

"The sub-treasury reminds me of an Irishman who had a yard full of poultry and one duck. When he came out with a basket of corn to feed the fowls he noticed that the duck gobbled up most of the corn with his broad bill.

"Be-dad, I'll put you on the same footing with the rest of them," he said.

He caught the duck and trimmed its bill to a sharp point so that it could only pick up one grain of corn at a time. Thompson said that was the way he would like to fix the sub-treasury, so that everybody would get their share.

He rode through the country and made friends with rural families, and talked to the women and children. Most of the men voted for him. That was before the day of woman suffrage.

Over near Easley Milton Mauldin had a large Grist Mill and wagon shop near "Mauldin's Mountain (later called Byar's Mountain). Along in the 1850's his eldest son Joab Mauldin took wagon trains loaded with produce to Hamburg and sold wagons and produce. George's Creek, Briggs, Hunts, Mayfields and every community had its interests, and its neighboring church.

In the Fall and Spring there were many droves of hogs, sheep and cattle coming from Tennessee through North Carolina and down through the Pickens County area to Augusta and Charleston. The farmers looked forward to disposing of part of their corn crops by selling it to the Drovers at the feeding stations. It took a lot of corn to feed four or five hundred hogs and wagon loads of it would be scattered on the ground for them at each camping place.

The Drovers were usually a rough lot and consumed a great deal of whiskey that the men brought hidden in the loads of corn. Some of them brought banjos and they would sit around the camp fires at night singing of romance and adventure. Some of their songs were the famous old mountain ballads which their ancestors had brought from England, Ireland, and Scotland, and others they composed as they traveeld.

Old books and newspapers tell us of one they often sang, especially if they happened to camp near an Inn when a square dance was coming up. It began like this: "Hog Drovers, hog drovers, hog drovers, we aire, Come courtin' your daughters, so young and so fair." And "Barbara Allen" was another tune that lingered after they were gone.

HAMBURG

Hamburg, South Carolina, now a dead town, and the site changed to North Augusta, was connected with the history of Pickens County in a strange way, It was the trade center that furnished a market for the surplus produce, the surplus output of shops and grist mills of the up country.

Two or three times a year wagoners would take loads of anything saleable they had to sell for cash or to barter for commodities that could not be obtained nearer home.

The establishment of the town Hamburg was the dream of one man, a German named Henry Schultz, and he named it for his home town in Germany.

He came to Augusta about 1806, when he was a very

young man. He had worked on a river boat from Savannah to Augusta until he saved $510, then he purchased a small boat for himself and ran his own business. He was a man of thrift and judgment and for several years everything he did seemed to prosper, but in the end he lost everything he possessed and died a penniless and bitter old man.

But in his young days he was a dreamer. He looked across the river from Augusta to the South Carolina side and saw great fields of corn, but he visualized a town there in-stead of a cornfield and he worked and planned to make his dream come true. In July 1821 he started building Hamburg, his own town. He built homes and stores and warehouses. When his funds gave out he appealed to the South Carolina Legislature for a loan, and on account of the remarkable progress he had made, and the possibility of the trade it might have with Charleston over the new railroad they were building, they loaned him $50,000 tax free for five years.

Schultz continued to progress. He built a mansion for himself in which he entertained royally. He established the Hamburg Bank, and a newspaper called the "Hamburg Journal." When the railroad was extended into Augusta, and other railroads were built to the upper part of the State his business began to decline, and the Augusta Canal, by-passing the rapids in the Savannah River completed his downfall, along in the late 1850's.

Before then one firm alone at Hamburg handled more than $200,000 a year in merchandise. Cotton shipping accounts were more than a $1,000,000 a year. Schultz claimed a great deal of unfairness from the business leaders of Augusta and died hating them. He requested to be buried in a standing position with his back toward Augusta to show his everlasting contempt for them.

Chapter Eight

There was fierce political strife along sectional lines in the decade prior to 1860. From the framing of the Federal Constitution in 1778 there had been two schools of political thought. One stood for extreme State's Rights and the other stood for a strong National Government of centralized power. The South clung to State's Rights. Abolitionists had grown in favor in the North, and like the Communists of our day they were getting in their work wherever they could. They were constantly trying to stir up trouble among the Negroes.

A statement in the Keowee Courier June 9, 1849 said: "We have been informed by several Post Masters in Pickens District that almost every mail brings a number of abolition documents addressed to individuals in this vicinity. How do the abolitionists obtain the names and addresses of people in this isolated section? Do we have traitors among us who are selling their birth right?"

The storm that had been brewing burst with fury during the Presidential campaign of 1860 in which Lincoln and Douglas were the standard bearers of the conflicting parties.

Lincoln was carried by the non-slave holding states, and the proposed "Crittendon Compromise" by Senator Crittendon of Kentucky was rejected. This measure proposed the re-establishment of the Missouri Compromise of 1820, which advocated slavery below a certain boundry. Pickens County men were keeping up with the news.

Talk of secession had reoccurred in South Carolina for years. These last events brought the crisis. Committees of South Carolina men from the up-country met in the Baptist Church in Columbia December 17, 1860 to make their final decision.

Those from Pickens District were: Andrew F. Lewis, Robert A. Thompson, William Hunter, William S. Gresham, and John Maxwell.

On December 20, 1860 these men met with other South Carolina Committees in Charleston, S. C. and the Ordianance of Secession was unanimously adopted by South Carolina. By June 1861 the other Southern States had come into the Confederacy and a Confederate Capitol was established at Montgomery, Alabama with Jefferson Davis of Mississippi, President; and Alexander H. Stevens of Georgia, Vice-President.

A new Government was formed within a few months. A new Constitution was framed, with executive, legislative, and judicial departments.

Francis W. Pickens, grandson of Gen. Andrew Pickens, became Governor of South Carolina in 1860. He put forth every effort to see that the soldiers were properly organized and instructed before they were called into battle.

This statement appeared in the "Blue Ridge Herald," Walhalla, S. C. July 9, 1861: "For the purpose of organization and instruction I designate 'Light Wood Springs' near Columbia or a proper location near Aiken for the establishment of Camps. Each Company, after an accurate roll of its members, and certificates of its officers shall return to the Camp nearest their home until they are called into Battalions and Regiments.—Francis W. Pickens, Gov. of S. C."

Army training was more inadequate then than now, but thanks to the County Muster Grounds, the men knew how to march and shoot when they went into Service.

As mentioned before, the area that is now Pickens County had many Muster Grounds. They were as follows: "Jones, at Pumpkintown, Eastatoe, Crow Creek, Hagood's, Hunter's, O'Dell's, Cooley's, and Pickensville, which was the largest of them all. Some one of them was convenient to every community, and some were used only for community practice. Dacusville men trained at Pickensville. Hunter's was on the north side of Wolf Creek, west of Pickens. It was a battalion ground where companies from the smaller grounds came together for practice in loading and firing cannon. A Mr. Keith was accidentally killed there by a cannon explosion some years before the Civil War. Homemade ginger bread and apple cider took the place of the present peanut butter sandwiches and Coca-Colas for light refreshments. Somebody in the community always furnished a "Ginger-bread Wagon."

Scattered facts and traditional bits of local history handed down by early citizens are about the only available records for Pickens County's life behind the lines during the 1860's. The list of Confederate Soldiers on file in the Pickens County Court House is incomplete because so many of the men went with companies organized at Old Pickens, Anderson, and Greenville. We are told that Pickens County sons were very patriotic and many were ready to enlist by the Fall of 1861. Others went as the calls came, even the sixteen year old boys near the end of the conflict

Four organized companies of Infantry went from the present Pickens County in the spring of 1861. They were under command of Captains Hamilton Boggs, Wylie Hollingsworth, J. M. Stewart, and R. H. Y. Griffin.

Captain Griffin's company was the first to leave Pickens County. They assembled in front of the Griffin home which is on Ann Street in Pickens now (Mrs. G. G. Christopher's 1958). It was a farm home then surrounded by woods and fields. The Griffin and Hollingsworth companies were soon attached to the 4th South Carolina Regiment. Captain R. H. Y. Griffin was killed in the Battle of Seven Pines.

Captain J. M. Stewart's company met at Hunter's Muster Ground. They joined the 22nd South Carolina Regiment. Captain Boggs' company was attached to the 22nd South

Carolina Rifles with John V. Moore as Colonel. A company
of Cavalry was organized by Alfred T. Clayton, as Captain.
This company joined Black's Regiment. Earle's Cavalry Company was composed partly of Pickens and partly of Greenville men. Some Pickens men went with the Fort Hill Guards,
and some with the Orr Rifles, from Anderson; and some went
with the Mountain Boys and Oconee Rifles from Old Pickens.
In July 1861 Capt. A. D. Gaillard formed Co. G 12th Regiment of South Carolina Infantry and some Pickens men
were in that. Some of the soldiers never came back, and some
came back minus a limb, as is the way in all wars.

Our histories tell us that the first shot of the War was
fired from Morris Island to intercept the "Star of the West"
as she came to Fort Sumter. But a traditional story has always persisted in Pickens County that one of our own men
named "William Mauldin" fired the first shot from Fort
Moultrie in the attack on Fort Sumter, which was the initial
engagement of the War, beginning hostilities in earnest.

William Mauldin's home was near the present town of
Easley. He went through the War and died at home. He was
buried in a family graveyard near his home, but about fifty
years later his body was removed to the Easley Cemetery and
interred with military honors.

Many families gave two or three sons to the Confederacy, some gave five or six. Among these were the Fosters
of Peter's Crek, the Loopers of Cross Roads, and the Boldings
of the Six Mile area. Joseph Looper gave each of his six sons
a good horse, without cost to the Government when they
joined the Cavalry. One of the boys was wounded and died
in a hospital in Virginia. His wife went to Virginia to nurse
him and when he died she brought his body home. Greenville was the nearest railroad station and when she arrived
the problem of transportation for the body confronted her.
Greenville was only a country town then. Finally, she found
one of the Cross Roads men who had come to Greenville in

an ox-cart and that was the way they brought the young soldier back to Cross Roads for burial.

Some Pickens County men spent weary months in Prison Camps. There were many deaths on the battlefields, some from wounds, some from pneumonia and other diseases. Many were never brought home. Many are buried in Confederate sections of cemeteries in the North among rows of small white slabs where others shared the same fate. Some are buried in Virginia and some in far-away Wisconsin.

A few men hid out to keep from going to war, and some deserted and hid in the mountains to run bootleg liquor stills. But their former neighbors thought of them with scorn, and their descendants were ostracized for years afterwards.

But the Union Army had deserters too. Through the years a traditional story has been told of such a man who hid in a cave on the side of Caesar's Head and picked up what food he could round the cabins in the Table Rock Cove at night. To disguise himself and frighten those who might come near his hiding place he would wrap himself in a sheet and walk back and forth on a ledge of the mountain on moonlight nights. The story soon spread that that section of the mountains was haunted. The nervous tension of the times had its effect on people and most of our early settlers were superstitious. Many old Negro women professed fortune telling and for a small remuneration they would read the palms of lovestick girls whose sweethearts had gone to War.

Some had the old New England fear of witches and told stories of how the suspected witches could turn themselves into animals and harm their enemies. One of these traditional stories was often repeated. "An old Pickens County man was repairing his rail fence when a rabbit got in his way. He threw his hammer at the rabbit and missed it, but something strange happened to the muscles of his eyes and he could never lift them again. Always after that he was pointed out as the man who was bewitched by a rabbit. And some were sure they knew the counterpart of the rabbit."

One of tht Craigs in the Keowee Valley owned a slave child who became known as "Keowee Susan". She was considered a phenomenon by some, and others thought she was bewitched. When she was about six years old she started turning white in spots and as time went on the spots spread until she was almost completely white.

The burdens borne by Pickens County women at home during the War were as great as any in the South. Crops must be planted and tended and if there were no slaves, which was usually the case, the women and children had to do the work.

There were no free schools, and few of any kind. Neighborhood attempts were made to teach their children elementary reading, writing, spelling and arithmetic.

The Southern women of 1860-1865 should be an inspiration to women of any day. Willingly and proudly they gave their men to the cause of saving the South, and filled with patriotic zeal they managed things at home. There were no alloment checks to look forward to—everything was their responsibility. Substitutes had to be used for almost everything. It was substitutes or nothing. The South was totally unprepared for war. Most of the factories were in the North. Coffee passed out of memory—all kinds of parched grains were used. Flour and sugar became unknown quantities. It was corn meal for bread, and molasses and honey for sweetening. Everybody tried to raise hogs and chickens. There was no substitute for salt. The floors of old smokehouses were scraped and boiled to get the dirt out of the salt. Ashes of corn cobs was used for making soda. After these ashes stood in water several hours the water would be clear, and one part of it mixed with two parts sour milk made very good bread.

Soap was made by adding drippings from the ash-hopper to waste grease. An ash-hopper was standard equipment in every back yard. Corn made into big-hominy (often called lye hominy) was a favorite dish with some. It was considered especially good with ham gravy.

There was no oil for lamps. (Electricity was unknown). Candle molds were a necessity in every home and candles were made in the kitchens. What was known as a Confederate Candle was a cloth string dipped in tallow and wound on a stick. The poorer homes used pine torches for lights.

Neatly trimmed thorns were used for pins and large seeds covered with cloth were used for buttons. The loss of a needle was a disaster. All of the women knew how to spin and weave to help clothe their families.

Letters were written to the men at the front but sometimes it was months before they received them, if ever. And the home folks did not get mail often. Envelopes were very scarce. Letters were usually folded and stuck with wax. They paid the Post Master and he made a "Povisional Mark" instead of stamp.

But the people at home worked together and played together. If no recent sorrow prevented, the mothers in a community would sometimes call the young people together for a singing or a play-party. And then all ages met at corn-shuckings, log-rollings, and barn buildings for the old men and young boys while the women cooked supper and had a quilting party.

There was much merriment around the corn piles and all of them sang together—"Barbara Allen—Seeing Nelly Home —and the Bonnie Blue Flag." These workings and parties combined were often the beginning of romances. After the work was finished they would go inside to a plain bountiful supper, and then play "Steal Partners, Hurly Burly—Skate Around the Ocean, and Square Dancing." Sometimes there was the music of a "fiddle" or a banjo, sometimes the parties were made lively by the songs and dance calls of the young people.

One old lady left a written account of a corn-shucking she had attended as a child. She told about a wedding party that came by while they were at the corn pile and how the group cheered the bride and groom as they passed. The groom was Mr. W. B. Allgood, home from Army duty on a furlough and his bride had been Miss Fannie Rogers, both well known natives of Pickens County. For almost a half century after the War Mr. Allgood was known on the streets of Pickens as an honored Confederate soldier.

There was no great wealth and no dire poverty in the present Pickens County before the War. It was a land of comfortable homes. The Calhouns in the lower part of the county, some people at Old Pickens, Pickensville, and some around Oolenoy owned slaves. These Negroes worked faithfully and well for their white families while the men were away from home. They were sympathetic and kind when trouble came, and few were ever disloyal.

But four years is a long time and as the war went on starvation began to stare some of the Pickens County citizens in the face. Women and children of the poorer families often needed help. The Commissioners of the Poor were instructed to give special aid to the widows and children of Confederate soldiers.

But more trouble came when the War was over. Sherman's march did not come through Pickens County but gangs of robbers and marauders did. They took all of the horses that the women needed for farm work. They took all of the corn and wheat, and hams and side meat from the smoke-houses. They fed their horses in walnut and mahogany bureau drawers. They prowled through boxes of silver and keepsakes and took what they wanted. One lady had just finished making a dozen candles out of the last tallow on the place and they took them. She snatched one as they were going out the door to use if her family had sickness in the night.

The so called Yankees, did not march straight through Pickens County. They covered it generally several times to get what they might have missed on the first trip.

Dr. Bill Edens who lived at Pumpkintown tried to resist them when they took his horses and all of his meat and grain. He shot at them when they were leaving, and then hid in a clump of trees near the Oolenoy River. They came back and burned the house. The next year Dr. Edens made brick on his own place and built a sturdy two-story brick house that is still standing. The walls are very thick and the chimneys are a continuous part of the wall. The overhead beams and supports inside are hand hewn. After Dr. Edens died it passed to the Masters family and in 1958 belongs to Mr. and Mrs. Henry Trotter.

There are several old houses still standing around Pumpkintown. The best kept one of these is the Matthew Hendricks house now the home of his daughter, Mrs. J. I. Reece. It was formerly a log house, the home of Mr. Allen Keith. His daughter, Mrs. Hendricks, inherited her father's home and after her husband, Matthew Hendricks, came back from the Civil War he weatherboarded it over the logs and made it the first framed house in Pumpkintown.

Many stories are told of how the women and children and slaves tried to hide things from the Yankees. Some of the stories are humorous, now that we are past those trying days. One lady told of hiding a well cured country ham that they were saving until her husband's return. They took it to the woods and hung it high in a tree. Unnoticed the family dog had followed them to the woods. When they went back to the house he took his stand under the tree and howled long and mournfully. They were never able to entice him back to the house. They finally gave up and took the ham to the smokehouse where the Yankees got it when they came through the next day.

If only a few of the prowlers had come through it would

have been easier but they kept coming for several months at unexpected times. It left its mark on the people and it was years after the War and the bitter days of Reconstruction before some of them could tolerate Northern people. One old lady in Pickens never would. In after years when her grandchildren brought home school friends who lived above the Mason and Dixon Line she would keep to the privacy of her room. She loved the sentimental poetry of the old South and the following poem by some forgotten author was framed and hanging on her wall:

"The heart knows no forgetting, and within her silent halls
Where the fragrant incense rises and the inner sunlight falls,
Hang the swords and rusty scabbards with the coats of faded
*   gray;*
And perfumed with myrrh and aloes All the flags are laid
*   away."*

MANY YEARS LATER

Under the stress of hard times and the bitter days of reconstruction there was no effort made to honor the Confederate soldiers in Pickens County until after the turn of the century. About 1901 the late Waddy T. McFall organized the Garvin Camp United Confederate Veterans, a county wide organization, and Mrs. Emma Ambler Gilreath organized the Pickens Chapter United Daughters of Confederacy.

In 1903 the U.D.C. (United Daughters of the Confedecy) set aside June 3rd (Jefferson Davis' birthday) as a day to honor the Confederate soldiers with an all day picnic on the Court House square. For forty years, without interruption, until the last of the old soldiers had passed away this was a special day in Pickens, and largely attended by citizens from every nook and corner of the county. One hundred and seventy-four veterans attended that first reunion. Old newspapers tell us that the picnic tables on the

Court House Square were "groaning" with their load of good things to eat. If Pickens didn't have a band they invited one from another town and they always played "Dixie," and "Tenting Tonight On the Old Camp Ground." There was always a noted speaker who held forth in the Court Room after he was introduced to the crowd by the Hon. James P. Carey, Sr., Judge T. J. Mauldin, or some other prominent local citizen. In later years of the celebration Dr. Rion McKissick and Dr. D. W. Daniel spoke for them, and they were frequently dismissed with a prayer by the Rev. D. W. Hiott. The Court House never held the crowd.

In 1927, at the 25th reunion, forty-three old soldiers were present out of sixty-three still living in the county.

Some of those who never failed to attend the picnic as long as they lived were: Capt. W. B. Allgood, Mr. W. R. (Pete) Price, Mr. Matthew Hendricks, Mr. Welborn Pickens, Mr. C. B. Finley, Mr. R. A. Bowen, Mr. Robert Stewart, Mr. J. M. Stewart, Mr. Elias Day, Mr. W. A. Lark, Mr. A. K. Edens, Mr. W. R. Garrett, Mr. D. H. Cassell, Mr. S. M. Looper, Mr. S. J. R. Robinson, Rev. J. E. Foster, Mr. W. N. Bolding, Mr. H. B. Hendricks, Mr. W. W. McWhorter, Mr. J. H. Porter, Mr. B. T. Dillard, Mr. T. H. Smith, Mr. W. T. O'Dell, Mr. John A. Durham, Mr. John Watson, Mr. John W. Thomas, Mr. Charlie Childers, Mr. W. T. Aiken, Mr. A. C. Masters, Mr. J. A. Griffin, Mr. John Julian, Mr. G. W. Trotter, Mr. W. T. Nalley, Mr. W. H. McDaniel, Mr. J. G. Powers, Mr. Matthew Benjamin, Mr. J. T. Long, Mr. J. Chappell, and many others whose names are hard to read on the old faded newspapers.

Several of the old men lived to be more than ninety. Mr. Matthew Hendricks lived to be 102. Many of them lived to see their country pass through two more wars.

FROM 1865 TO 1875

Chapter IX

In 1865 when the War was over and the pitiful remnants of the Confederate Army were finding their way home Congress met to form Reconstruction plans and a bitter quarrel ensued.

President Johnson wanted to set up a system of State Governments to let each Southern State work out is own problems. But Congress said the voting status of the Southern states had been destroyed. They expressed the belief that Negroes in the South could only be protected by letting them have political rights.

In 1866 Congress passed a bill that all Southern States must ratify the Fourteenth Amendment. Tennessee was the only State that ratified it. The other Southern Sates stood together.

In March 1867 Congress passed over President Johnson's vetoes what they called Reconstruction Acts. The Southern States that had refused to ratify the Amendment were placed under military rule. They were divided into five military districts, two states to a District, with a General of the United States Army in command of each District. It was the duty of this General to supervise the organization in each state to take the place of Johnson's form of Government. The real purpose was to destroy the Democratic Party in the South. In October 1867 Gen. Daniel E. Sickles who was in command of North and South Carolina, ordered a complete registration of both the Negro and white races. In the South Carolina registration they counted 78,982 Negroes and 43,-346 white men. There was no woman suffrage at that time. The Democrats condemned the Reconstruction Acts. Prominent South Carolina Democrats headed by Gen. Wade Hampton issued a statement in 1867 in which they alleged that the Reconstruction Acts placed South Carolina politically and socially under the heel of its Negro citizens, and that the Radicals were not seeking justice for the Negro but only wanted to embarrass the whtie citizens.

Addressing some of the citizens of Pickens District with whom he had served in the Army Gen. Hampton said: "As slaves the Negroes were faithful. Let's treat them as friends. The two races in the South understand each other and it is safe to say that if left alone they would work out their difficulties."

The Constitutional Convention assembled in Charleston January 14, 1868 to frame a Constitution and Civil Government. The Convention was dominated by Negroes and Federalists who had come into the State as agents and adventurers. Chamberlain made his first appearance in South Crolina at that Convention.

Robert K. Scott, the first Republican Governor of South Carolina had been a practicing physician in Ohio before the War. He attained the rank of Major General in the Union Army. More than half of the legislators elected with Scott were Negroes, and many of them were unable to read or write. As the first Governor to live in the Executive Mansion in Columbia Scott entertained Negroes and whites on terms of social equality.

The most tragic episodes in South Carolina occurred during Scott's administration. South Carolina became known as "The Prostrate State." It was readmitted to the Union on June 25, 1868.

Confederate money and bonds were worthless. If a family had a little gold money they hoarded it carefully.

Pickens District was divided into Pickens and Oconee Counties in January 1868, actually before South Carolina was accepted back into the Union. It was impossible to get a town charter for the new Court House town of Pickens at that unsettled time. And afterwards it was neglected until after the turn of the century. They continued with the 1847 charter acquired at Old Pickens, until 1908.

Pickens was one of the nine counties in the State that had few Negroes and it fared better for that reason. It had less carpet bag and scalawag trouble, and the Negro militia only rode through the county a few times. The local Negroes remained loyal to their former masters. They had little need for the Ku-Klux-Klan organization formed in some counties to combat the Negro "Loyal League," which was sponsored by Scott and Moses. By 1869 the Klan had almost ceased to exist on account of unscrupulous characters getting into it.

Pickens District was divided into Pickens and Oconee Counties and the new county kept the name "Pickens." The area west of Keowee River became "Oconee County" by a favorite Indian name of that section. The boundary between the two counties was established by an imaginary line first down the center of White Water and later Toxaway River, and then down the center of Keowee River to Ravenel's Bridge at Clemson. Then along the center of the highway toward Pendleton to the Anderson County line.

The Anderson County line formed the Southern boundary, the Saluda River the eastern boundary, and Table Rock, Mt. Pinnacle, Sassafras, and other mountins the northern boundary joining North Carolina.

The back moutains of Pickens County are a part of the Sumter National Forest and have sometimes been called the Switzerland of South Carolina on account of their scenic beauty. Sassafras Mountain, 3548 feet, is said to be the highest point in South Carolina. Mount Pinnacle is 3413 feet, and Table Rock is 3157 ft.

The following Commissioners were appointed to locate a place for the County seat, as near the center of the County as possible: James H. Ambler, J. E. Hagood, W. T. Field, Reese Bowen, James Lewis, and Thomas Price.

By proper surveys they discovered the center of the County was near the old Hagood Grist Mill. But the narrow wagon road that led through that section was very rough and they decided the location was too hilly and inaccessible. Then they went a mile south of the present Pickens, near old Bethlehem Church .They had heard that the Air Line Railroad was contemplating a survey of that ridge for a possible route through Pickens County.

But before the Commissioners made a final decision Elihu Griffin offered forty acres of his plantation for a town site. The land was designated, "for a Court House and Public Buildings." The offer was accepted. The land was in woods and a spot for the Court House was selected and cleared. Soon they began pulling stumps out of what was to be the Main Street of the new town of Pickens.

Bricks for the Court House were made locally and the building was finished in 1869. Mr. J. E. Hagood built a small frame law office where the City Hall now stands. It was used for all legal purposes and for a union Sunday School until the Court House was finished, then religious services were held in the Court Room until a small frame Methodist Church was built in 1871 on land donated by Esther Robinson Hagood (Mrs. J. E.)

The founders of Pickens lived in tents and log cabins until they could build permanent homes. A few of the houses at "Old Pickens" were torn down, moved to the new town and rebuilt. The most outstanding one of these was the J. E. Hagood home, which many years later belonged to his daughter (Miss Queen), Mrs. T. J. Mauldin. Others that were moved were the Thornley, Alexander, and Bruce Senior houses. Mr. and Mrs. P. McD. Alexander ran the first hotel in Pickens on the corner of Main Street opposite the (1958) Winn-Dixie Store. In a year or two Mrs. Alexander's health failed and they swapped homes with the Thornleys and moved to a frame cottage which stood where the present 1958. Mrs. T. L. Bivens Sr.'s residence stands. The Thornleys continued to run the hotel for many years. J. McD. Bruce built a home facing it. across the street where Winn-Dixie stands.

Miss Florence Morgan of Dacusville who married Mr. Holby Griffin of Pickens (the son of Elihu Griffin) was the first bride in Pickens and lived in the first new house. It is now (remodeled), the home of Mr. and Mrs. T. B. Lanham. 1958.

Some of the men who were prominently associated with the town and county lived on farms several miles out, where they owned nice farm homes. Among these were: J. H. Ambler, W. T. Field, Joab Mauldin, Reese Bowen, T. R. Price, H. J. Anthony, C. L. Hollingsworth at Twelve Mile and later Matthew Hendricks of Pumpkintown. I. H. Philpot of Dacusville was the first Probate Judge.

The first school in Pickens was a temporary affair, a brush arbor near the location of the present Presbyterian Church. Mrs. Goodlett, a lawyer's wife, was the first teacher.

The first school house was a log cabin where the Food Locker stands. Miss Sue Dickinson and Miss Vesta Mauldin were the first teachers. Miss Vesta Mauldin was the daughter of Joab Mauldin (Pickens County's first Sheriff), and she afterwards became the wife of W. T. McFall one of the leading merchants in Pickens for a number of years. Their descendants still live in Pickens.

Dr. Francis Miles was the first doctor in Pickens with an office in his home where the first Baptist Church stands (1958). Dr. J. D. Cureton was the first dentist.

Mr. Alonzo M. Folger was the first Post Master then J. T. Burdine and A. M. Morris next.

Mr. L. A Brown a cabinet and furniture maker made

many chests, tables, and beds for the first homes in Pickens And it was about that time when "ready made" coffins were advertised. Until then coffins had been made by loving friends after a death.

Mrs. E. Hughes had a dressmaking and tailoring business in a house on the East end of Pickens, "facing the Thornley Hotel," which at that time stood on the corner of Main Street. She advertised making clothes for "Men, women, and children." She also advertised "photography, and beautiful plush backed photograph albums, with heavy brass fasteners. Some of them "with muisc boxes in the back."

The Pickens Sentinel began publication in 1871 and has published continuously since that time. Once when the typesetter had a sore hand they only got out a single sheet. And once when paper was unavailable they published the weekly news on a folded sheet of lined tablet paper, but they kept going. D. F. Bradley and J. R. Holcombe were listed as the first Editor and Publishers, then the next year D. F. Bradley was alone, and in 1874 the paper was published by D. F. Bradley and R. A. Childs. Other changes came as the years passed. Once it became "the Sentinel Journal"—and then changed back to the Pickens Sentinel.

The new Pickens County floated a $100,000 bond issue to help build the Air Line Railroad. There was much discussion and wrangling about this at the time and several law-suits afterwards. Some of the states went into railroad building with sad results after their legislatures had authorized bond issues. Perhaps the Pickens County Commissioners and the Delegation took the long view, that a backwoods county would never become progressive without a railroad. And in time it paid off.

From the close of the War until 1872 Southern people lived through a period of fear and horror. Thaddeus Stevens, the Radical leader of the House of Representatives in Washington, and the author and promoter of the Reconstruction

Acts had a mulatto woman for his mistress and often boasted that he would "Africanize" the South. He planned the "Freedman's Bureau through which every ex-slave would obtain the gift of forty acres of land and a mule, and the rest of the white mens' land was to be sold to pay off the War debt. That was the period in which the Ku-Klux-Klan flourished in the South and did some good.

By 1873 a depression had struck the Nation which is comparable to the more recent 1929 crash. A great banking house in Philadelphia failed, stocks went down, thousands of men were laid off from work in the Northern states. The Nation wide scarcity of money inspired the formation of paper money which was called "greenbacks."

While the North was in so much trouble the pressure lightened some on the down-trodden South and Chamberlain became Governor of South Carolina, with great talk of reforms. The Negro situation was still bad but it seemed at a standstill.

The Freedman's Bureau had caused very little trouble in Pickens County. In the mountains above Pumpkintown several thousand acres of land was set aside for a colony of ex-slaves numbering about 300. The settlement was called "Liberia." They built a church and school called "Soapstone," on account of the layers of soapstone that crop out nearby. The Liberia Negroes spent their lives happily and peaceably on their little farms still showing friendliness and affection for their former masters in the Oolenoy area. And some of their descendants still live there. An older Negro church called "Nebo" is not far from the Oolenoy Church. It was started before the Civil War by the plantation owners for their slaves. It is well kept and well attended by the Negroes of that section and others who have moved away and still like to come back to their home church. Tomb is another, very old Negro church.

After the Air Line Railroad was built across the lower

half of Pickens County towns grew up along its path. Easley, Liberty, and Central were the first and later Norris and Calhoun, and two flag stops, Lathem and Croswell.

We see in the Pickens Sentinel October 16, 1873: "The depot at Easley Station has been completed and is now ready for the reception of freight. R. E. Holcombe, Esq. has been appointed Depot Agent."

The Easley depot was built only a few blocks from the old Mt. Olivet Camp Ground which became the site of Easley's first Methodist Church with a cemetery surrounding it.

J. R. Glazener was Easley's first Postmaster and ran a small store in connection with the Postoffice. Almost every week The Sentinel carried news of homes and businesses that were being built in Easley. Easley received its charter in 1874. And a Methodist minister, J. Q. Stockman, began teaching a small school there before the town was a year old. And soon "Clyde and Mote" were runnnig a hotel near the depot.

Liberty had a church and school at Salubrity Spring near the present town for many years before the railroad came through. And once the famous old teacher and preacher, John L. Kennedy taught school in a little building about where the Liberty depot now stands.

Mrs. Catherine Templeton had a beautiful plantation home. When the railroad came through she gave the right of way across her land. This gave her many desirable building lots and in a Pickens Sentinel of 1873 she describes these lots and offers them for sale, with the help of her sons-ni-law Addison Boggs, and S. M. Holcombe. R. E. Holcombe seems to have been the business manager of the sale. There are four Holcombes mentioned in the affairs of Pickens County in the 1870's: "W. E. Holcombe, R. E. Holcombe, S. M. Holcombe, and J. R .Holcombe. The relationship is not given.

The old Thomas Boggs house was built in 1817, as a

plantation home. The town of Liberty grew up around it. It was torn down in 1958. Liberty applied for a charter in 1875. The incorporate limits extended a mile in each direction from the depot which had been built by the citizens on the south side of the railroad. A "Liberty Hotel" which was run by J. J. Nix was advertised in The Sentinel in 1875. Later hotels were run by "Avenger, Willard, and Brown."

Some of the earliest names in Liberty were: "Templeton, Boggs, Willard, Brown, Smith, Holcombe, Chapman, Callaham, Hallum, Brown, Hunter, and Richardson.

John Hallum mentioned as one of the founders of old Pickensville in 1791 lived a mile or two south of Liberty. He died in 1813 and was buried in a family graveyard. His home burned. He was a Revolutionary soldier and held a land grant for 5000 acres on Eighteen Mile Creek. He has many descendants in Liberty and Pickens. He attended church at Carmel and his land joined the churchyard. He donated a piece of land across the road, facing the present Flat Rock Schoolhouse, for a slave graveyard. Mr. T. N. Hunter was his grandson. Mr. Hunter suffered the loss of his father by scalawags in the early reconstruction days. Mr. Nez Hunter, the father, had hired some of his willing ex-slaves to help gather the crops after he came home from the War and one moonlight night two horsemen rode up to the gate and called him out. Then without a word of explanation they shot him down and rode away.

The old Postoffice "Salubrity, which had existed for many years before the change of counties was moved into town and the name changed to the "Liberty Postoffice". Mr. John T. Boggs was the first Post Master, with Sam D. Stewart, assistant. It was in Mr. Stewart's home.

The first Sunday School in Liberty was organized in the little school house and the Rev. W. K. Boggs was the first teacher.

In a Pickens Sentinel, December 7, 1875 S. M. Holcombe advertised a general store: "I respectfully inform the citizens of Liberty, and Pickens County that I have opened a new and fresh stock of goods. Dry goods, boots and shoes, Hardware, crockery, lamps and kerosene oil, molasses and salt. I have just received 400 sacks of flour, 20 barrels of mackerel, plenty of sugar and coffee." And then in an added paragraph: "Wanted—1,000,000 shingles, and 10,000 bushels of corn—highest market prices paid.—S. M. Holcombe."

Central grew up near the old Garvin Post Office. It got the name "Central" because it was half way between Charlotte and Atlanta on the new Air Line Railroad. It was selected as a suitable place for the railroad shops, and a dining place for passengers and railroad men was established there. They could be served while the trains refueled. There were no dining cars on trains in that day.

Hester and Hester ran the first general store at Central. Before the first churches were built there were neighboring churches within three or four miles that the people attended. The first school was taught by a Mr. Broadus, a graduate of Furman. There were no free schools then. The following figures show the apportionment by the School Commissioners of the $4,929.00 allotted to Pickens County out of the appropriation of $300,000.00 for the State support of common schools for the fiscal year ending October 31, 1873:

"1st District—Pickensville—$788.40

2nd District—Salubrity—$569.30

(Central) 3rd District—Garvin—466.44

4th District—Easley—706.28

5th District—Pickens—964.32

6th District—Dacusville—$519.76

7th District—Pumpkintown—334.40

8th District—Eastatoe—700.00.

By the aid of the "Peabody Fund", a charitable award for schools in isolated communities, a school was established at Nine Times in the Eastatoe section of Pickens County. It ran ten months a year for three years, with John O. Wallace as Principal. The Sentinel gave the tuition, as follows: "Primary, $4, Intermediate $5, Advanced $7.50." Board was quoted as from five to seven dollars a month" in the best families."

At the same time this school was in session there were three churches in Eastatoe, established by the Baptist Mission Board. They were—"Cane Creek, Whitesides, and Bethel."

There were "protracted meetings" at every church in the County at some time during the summer if rains had not made the roads impassable.

Weather conditions were erratic then, as now. We are told of a seven inch snow that came in March and stayed on the ground for days. Sometimes there were "freshets" that washed away all the small plank bridges and damaged many grist mills.

Oolenoy Church had many faithful members over a wide area. John Chastain, M. Chastain, and the Rev. John Roper were its first pastors. Rev. John Roper served as pastor twenty-eight years without pay, except in produce from his members. He is buried there in the Oolenoy Church yard.

In July 1876 the Oolenoy Baptist Church established a set of By-Laws, as follows: "Ordinance 1. The Church shall elect on the first regular meeting in each year, a Council of at least five men, whose duty it shall be to control all matters coming under the jurisdiction—one of whom shall act as chairman, and they shall sit as a court to try all cases that may be brought before them for any trespass or misdemeanor that may be committed within the corporate limits of the church.

II. If any one tried by the council shall fail to comply

with the decision of the same, they shall be brought by the chairman before a higher court of trial.

III. The councils shall appoint two marshals who shall have power to appoint as many assistants as they deem necessary. It shall be the duty of the marshal to bring before the council any person or persons that shall violate any laws of the incorporation.

IV. Any one who will buy, sell, drink or give to any one intoxicating drinks within the corporate limits of the church, shall be subject to a fine not exceeding $25, nor less than $5 and costs.

V. Anyone using profane language, loud talking, or in any way disturbing the congregation or any part there of in time of Divine Service, Sabbath School, or any Religious Exercises shall be subject to a fine not exceeding $50, nor less than $5 and costs.

VII. Any person burying in the space laid off for church yard will be subject to a fine not exceeding $500, nor less than $100 and costs.

VIII All monies collected by fine, or otherwise by the Council shall be placed in the hands of the Treasurer of the Church and used for church purposes."

Many men who lived in isolated sections of the mountains made illicit whiskey and stealthily hauled it to local towns, and to Greenville to sell. They found this easier than hauling great loads of corn that they had raised in their fertile valleys.

To hinder this practice the State Government allowed licensed Government Distilleries to be established, and they appointed Revenue officers to keep on the alert for illicit distillers. The old newspapers frequently reported arrests that had been made. One of these items in 1876 is headed: "Revenue Raid: Deputy Collector E. H. Barton, with a detachment of Maj. Wagoner' force brought fourteen prisoners from the mountains of our county last Tuesday. They had been arrested for illicit distilling and were lodged in jail."

In another paper: "Revenue Officers Maloney and Gary captured an ox team with twenty or thirty gallons of contraband whiskey on Friday night. The driver got away."

And there were many such cases in various parts of the county.

Along in the 1870's the County Commissioners sold the Poor Farm near Old Pickens to Daniel Hughes for $2500. He had been the steward of it for a long time. They purchased Mr. B. F. Robertson's farm on Twelve Mile about three miles west of the new Court House for $3000, and Mr. Robertson gave about 200 bushels of corn and a quantity of shingles and loose lumber in the trade.

There wasn't much social life except Grange picnics, all day singings, and quilting parties in Pickens County.

At one of the Grange picnics an old lady who was known as "Aunt Polly Williford" displayed a most unique and unusual quilt which she called "Grandmother Bowers Album Quilt." It was gotten up as a family record of the Bowers family. It began with Polly Bowers, mother of Job Bowers, and was completed just after the War (Civil War). It gave a complete list of children, grandchildren, and great-grandchildren. Trees were appliqued on squares. The 1st tree had 13 limbs to represent the number of children in that family. On the end of each limb was a flower with a child's name embroidered on it. And so on through the 4th generation, each tree having the number of limbs in that family. The total number of names on the quilt when it was finished was 242.

The "Farmer's Grange" had been introduced into Pickens County in 1873. It soon became popular, with a club in each community. Those who asked, what is a Grange? were told: "It makes every neighborhood a member of a National

Organization known as the Patrons of Husbandry. It heals the wounds of the unfortunate. It unites by strong ties those who have been strangers. It is an agricultural institution that seeks to obtain for its members the highest prices for their produce." The social part of it also helped the women to exchange ideas of cooking, sewing, canning, and quilting. But we have never heard that the "Album Quilt" had any followers.

But the women did not take all the honors for new, and unusual handiwork. Col. Robert E. Bowen, who at that time was a member of the Legislature from Pickens County, secured a patent to last seventeen years for an Improved Cotton Planter he had invented, on August 12, 1873.

The Planter was so constructed that it opened the furrow, dropped the seed, and covered them in one operation. It was arranged with a lever to cut off the flow of seed when desired, and in turning corners.

Col. Bowen planted his entire crop with the machine that year and was ready to put it on the market.

On Sept. 11, 1873 a notice appeared in The Sentinel: "The Colored Element And The Grange." It stated that heretofore the colored element had not been known in the Grange and discussed the question as to whether such a thing would be allowed in Pickens County. It further stated:

"Here in our county where the 'Patrons of Husbandry' is flourishing no application for such has been received, but in Arkansas and Missouri the crisis is at hand." Nothing was done.

Muster Grounds had not been reactivated since the War but there was a Rifle Club in each of the eight Townships of Pickens County, which were: "Eastatoe, Pumpkintown, Hurricane, Garvin (changed to Central), Liberty, Pickens, Easley, Dacusville." Rifle Clubs had been organized for the protection of homes and families. Although the general atmosphere of Pickens County was peaceful there was still much to be feared and dreaded in the management of State affairs.

An item about the new Air Line Railroad at that time, Sept. 11, 1873, stated: "Two first rate passenger trains are running daily between Atlanta and Charlotte, one going in either direction. A train now leaves Greenville at 12 A.M., runs to Toccoa on the Georgia side, and returns the same evening, arriving in Greenville between six and seven P.M., making connections at both places with the trains from Atlanta and Charlotte. The train passes Easley Station going to Toccoa City, at one P.M., and on the return trip at Six P.M. We mention this so that if any of our citizens desire to go in either direction they may catch the train at Easley, the only stopping place in Pickens County."

The new Railroad was making a good impression on the business men of the County and various appeals were being made to the citizens for other railroads. A narrow gauge railroad called the "Sassafras Gap Railroad" was mentioned in every issue of the paper and many meetings were held to promote it.

On June 5, 1873, a Railroad meeting was held in the Court House at Pickens by interested citizens from all over the County in the interest of the "Augusta and Chicago Short Line Railroad."

"On motion, Col. S. D. Goodlett was called to the Chair, and D. F. Bradley was elected Secretary.

"Col. Goodlett spoke as follows: 'Our County with its vast undeveloped resources only needs sufficient Railroad facilities to bring its fair hills and valleys the wealth that is rightfully theirs, " After several lengthy speeches the following standing Committee of ten was appointed: "T. H. Russell, Thos. Rogers, R. E. Bowen, C. L. Hollingsworth, W. A. Lesley, Dr. A. J. Anderson, J. W. Brown, W. H. Hester, J. B. Clayton, and James H. Hendricks." These men retired for a few minutes and then presented the following report:

"Whereas a meeting was recently held in Augusta, Ga. of the friends of a railroad enterprise known as the "Chicago and Augusta Short Line Railroad;" and whereas from the spirit evinced at that meeting, and the high character of the men promoting it, we are considering the claims of competing routes, on the score of practicality, directness, and cheapness of construction. We believe that Sassafras Gap presents the lowest depression in the chain of the Blue Ridge Mountains, lying on a direct line from Lexington, Ky. to Augusta, Ga.

The following Resolutions were made: That the said Committee of ten open correspondence with Railroad Officials and others who had taken an active interest in this development. That they have the proceedings of this meeting published in the following newspapers: "The Pickens Sentinel, The Anderson Intelligencer, Abbeville Press and Banner, Edgefield Advertiser, Augusta Chronicle, Beaufort Paper, Port Royal Advocate, and the papers of Asheville, N. C."

1. Marker at Pickensville. Henry Lark gave land. 2. Marker at Keowee Village. 3. Pleasant Alexander home at Old Pickens. 4. Pickens in 1920. 5. Site of Keowee Village. 6. Marker at Fort Prince George Site. 7. General Andrew Pickens.

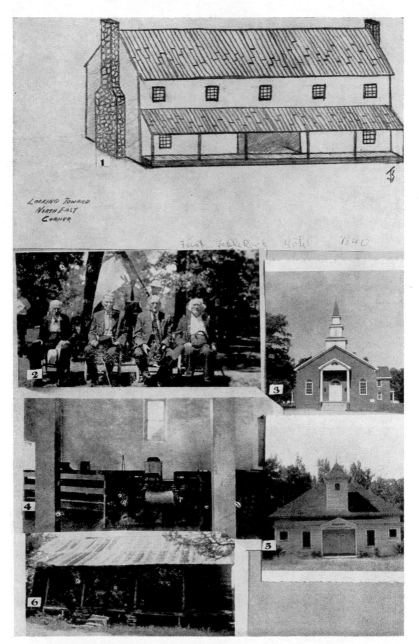

1. First Hotel at Table Rock sketched by Mrs. Sutherland. 2. Confederate Soldiers. 3. New Church at Oolenoy. 4. Inside of Old church. 5. Old Oolenoy School—Now Community House. 6. Old Jones Home.

1. Dr. Bill Edens Home at Pumpkintown. 2 Church at Old Pickens.
3. Mrs. J. I. Reece's Home at Pumpkintown (Old Matthew Hendricks
Home). 4. Aiken Home at Oolenoy. 5. Pickens Main Street Long
Ago. 6. Keowee River. 7. Mrs. Queen (T.J.) Mauldin's Home in
Pickens.

Original drawing by. Glenn A. Cannon.

1. Original Elihu Griffin Home in Pickens. 2. Carmel Church.
3. Piedmont Institute in Pickens.

1. Chapman's Covered Bridge Across Keowee River. 2. Table Rock, Lake and Lodge. 3. Church At Old Pickens. 4, 5, 7 Old Grist Mills Sketched by Glenn Cannon. 6. Revolutionary Soldier's Marker at Pickens Chapel. 8. Bridge Over Keowee River. 9. Present Court House. 10. First Court House in Pickens (1869). 11. First 4-H Club Encampment at Rocky Bottom.

1. Negro Home in Liberia. 2. Soapstone Church (Negro) 3. Old Stone Church. 4. Foster Keith Hotel at Table Rock. 5. Old Boggs Home at Liberty—One of the Oldest Houses in Liberty.

1, 2, 3, 6. Cyclone at Six Mile. 4. Six Mile Hospital. 5. Dr. and Mrs. Peek and Nurses at Six Mile. 7. J. E. Hagood Home Moved From Old Pickens. 8. Frank McFall Home at Pickens.

PICKENS MAYOR AND CITY COUNCIL, HEALTH OFFICERS, CHIEF OF POLICE, AND ASSISTANT
7, Mayor B. B. Laboon, 1, J. A. Peek, 2, J. L. Valley, M.D., 3, Dr. F. S. Porter, 4, B. F. Parsons, 5, W. T. Jones, 6, J. R. Ashmore,
9, L. F. Robinson, 8, J. F. Hays, 10, G. W. Corbin, 11, J. N. Hollum, 12, H. A. Nealey, Chief of Police.

EASLEY CITY COUNCIL
1, J. M. Jameson, Mayor.   7, Chief Police, A. S. Jameson.

CITY COUNCIL OF CENTRAL
1, B. J. Johnson, Mayor, 2, J. T. Gassaway, 3, J. W. Brock, J. D. Boggs, 5, E. B. Stephens, 6, J. F. Castleberry

Main Street Of Pickens — 1907

Chapter X

A feature article in the Anderson "Intelligencer" in 1875 told how quickly the town of "Old Pickens" had degenerated after the Court House moved away. In seven years there was very little left to show where a thriving country town with comfortable, happy homes had once stood. For instance: "One lot of two acres on which was a good dwelling and store room attached sold for $20."

The jail and Court House and many dwellings had been torn down and moved away but the old hotel was still standing, minus its doors and windows which gave it a gloomy, and ghostly appearance on moonlight nights. About five white families and a few negroes were living there and a man from "Seneca City" had started a general store which seemed to be doing well.

The old brick church which had been established for Presbyterians had lately been incorporated in a Methodist Mission of the South Carolina Conference.

A Masonic Notice in an early issue of the Pickens Sentinel said: "Keowee Lodge No. 79 A.F.M. has moved to the new town of Pickens and established a place there to meet at six O'clock P.M. on Saturday before the full moon."

In January 1874 the following Masonic Officers were installed by Keowee Lodge No. 79 A.F.M.:

E. H. Bates, W.M., J. R. Holcombe, S.W., R. A. Child, J.W, W. T. Field, Treas., R. A. Bowen, Tyler, W. T. Bowen, Sec., R. R. Todd, S.D., T. J. Bowen, J.D., O. H. C. Smith and Taylor O'Dell, stewards.

An address was delivered by the Rev. Fletcher Smith, first preacher in Pickens.

The Granges were often mentioned in the Sentinel, and picnics and socials were held by the members that created a fine spirit of fellowship among the citizens of Pickens County.

In 1874 the names of some of the Grange Officers were printed in the paper, as follows: "Pickens—R. E. Bowen, Master; J. B. Clayton, Overseer; C. L. Hollingsworth, Lecturer; T. H. Russell, Chaplain; D. F. Bradley, Treasurer; James M. McFall, Secretary; R. A. Bowen, Steward; R. R. Todd, Asst. Steward; W. P. Price, Gate Keeper; Mrs. S. E. Mears, Lady Asst. Steward; Mrs. T. H. Russell, Ceres; Mrs. M. L. Oliver, Flora; Mrs. D. F. Bradley, Pomona.

Easley was not mentioned in this paper but Pickensville gave this list: "J. B. Griffin, M; Laban Mauldin, O; E. A. Russell, L; T. W. Russell, S; Jacob Pickel, Chap.; G. W. McClanahan, A.S.; Stephen B. Watson, Treasurer; L. C. Neal, Sec.; C. M. Watson, G.K.; Mrs. Laban Mauldin, Ceres; Miss Sallie Oates, Pomono; Miss Mattie Pickel, Flora; Mrs. L. C. Neal, L.A.S. Easley and George's Creek had flourishing organizations.

Liberty gave the following list: A. T. Clayton, M; Thos. Parkins, O; W. K. Boggs, L; Neal Singleton, Steward; Marcus Boggs, Asst. Steward; Samuel Stewart, Treasurer; W. R. Hollingsworth, Secretary; Clayton Smith, GK; Miss Hennie Chamblin, Ceres; Miss Mattie Boggs, Pomona; Mrs. M. A. Clayton, Flora; Mrs. Martha Hollingsworth, Lady Asst. Steward.

A County meeting was held at the Court House once a year and committees from each Grange in the County attended and discussed new rules for adoption. They were learning new methods of agriculture, and they were learning to organize and pull together.

At one County meeting the following representatives were mentioned: "J. J. Lewis, J. K. Kirksey, Pickens; M. D. Edens, Twelve Mile; Van S. Jones, Pumpkintown; W. G.

Field, J. R. Latham, Dacusville; Laban Mauldin, Dr. L. C. Neal, Pickensville; J. R. Glazner, Easley; J. R. Zachary, Holly Springs; J. W. Lawrence, Six Mile; G. W. Boroughs, Prater's Community; Mr. A. Briggs and Mr. S. James, George's Creek, and James McKinney, Eastatoe.

Feeling ran high when a notice appeared in the paper that the University of South Carolina had been practically opened to the colored race. Most of the teachers had resigned. And then the Institution at Cedar Springs in Spartanburg County for the education of the deaf, dumb, and blind was thrown wide open to negroes. The students were instructed in the same classes and served at the same tables. And all at the expense of the white tax-payers of the State.

All of these things were discussed at the Grange meetings and Democratic Clubs began forming. There were eight townships in the County and by 1875 it was announced that four of them were completely organized. With the Grange members as a nucleus it was not hard to get the people together, and by 1876 there were strong Democratic clubs in the eight townships.

There were a few Republicans in Pickens County, and some were prominent business men who claimed that their aim was to clean up the Republican Party and teach the negroes how to vote for good men. Some thought they were trying to keep on good terms with the men in power to get better public offices. Perhaps they were looking ahead.

In the latter part of 1875 the leading Democrats of South Carolina had started making plans. Some of them held a meeting in Columbia and counselled together. Before the next election they would have no open tickets for candidates, but a selected list of men who had proven to be South Carolina's strongest and best citizens. They must select a Democratic Governor—a real Southerner.

They all agreed on Gen. Wade Hampton for Governor; Gen. James Conner, Attorney General; Col. W. D. Simpson,

Lt. Governor; Gen. Johnson Hagood, Comptroller General; R. M. Simms, Secretary of State; Hugh S. Thompson, Commissioner of Education, and E. W. Moise, Adjutant and Inspector General.

Daniel H. Chamberlain had been elected Goveronr of South Carolina on the Republican ticket. He was a native of Massachusetts, and had been the lieutenant of a negro regiment in the Federal Army during the War He was a graduate of Yale and an able lawyer He was said to be a handsome man with a strong personality. He was shrewd, calculating, and contradictory. His character has never been completely analyzed. He claimed to be a reformer who would do great things for the South, but at the same time he appointed corrupt people to responsible positions in the State's government, and often incited negroes to acts of violence.

The depression of 1873 left little time for prejudice in the North and the better part of the population was ready to forget the War and move ahead. The New York newspapers carried editorials describing the shameful condition of politics in South Carolina. They commented that the Nation should not tolerate it and that the Government of the Southern States should be put into he hands of inelligent Southern men. In the election of 1874 the Democrats gained a majority in Congress.

Many Republicans, white and black, in South Carolina did not believe Chamberlain capable of becoming a reformer. The tide was turning against him. An independent group of Republicans was formed with Judge John T. Green of Sumter as their candidate for the next Governor, and a Charleston negro, Martin R. Delaney, for Lt. Governor. (Delaney was said to be the grandson of two African Chiefs).

After several negro riots, one at Hamburg and one at Ellenton in Aiken County, and what was known as the "Cainhoy Massacre" in Charleston Chamberlain made an appeal to the President of the United States, Ullyses S. Grant, tor more United States Troops to be sent to South Carolina. The Ku-Klux-Klan had almost stopped by that time, but Chamberlain feared the power of the Rifle Clubs, which he had tried to stop unsuccessfully, and there was a new organization called "Red Shirts" where each man wore a bright red shirt and patrolled the roads on public days to terrorize the scalawags and negroes who were giving offense.

President Grant answered the appeal for Troops by sending, "all Troops available in the Military District of the Atlantic."

Pickens County resented this as much as any county in the State although their negro population was small and reasonably peaceable. It might cause trouble from outside forces.

Slowly but surely the Democratic Clubs had grown in each of the eight Townships of Pickens County. The Grange organizations had no doubt helped to bring this to pass. While they were primarily agricultural in their intent and purpose they had brought groups together and politics had been freely discussed at their meetings.

Gen. Wade Hampton passed the word to all Democratic leaders in the State to urge their Clubs to submit to martial law if necessary and work out their problems quietly. The National Democratic Party regarded South Carolina as submissive under the heel of the Republicans by that time. While Chamberlain talked so constantly of making reforms some of the Democratic citizens doubted that a Democratic candidate could beat him in the next election; but a movement to restore the State to at least part of is original glory moved steadily forward.

Pickens County men took a big hand in promoting Gen. Wade Hampton for Governor of South Carolina. Hampton's War record gave the Democrats confidence in his ability and his family for generations back had been men and women of integrity. He was at his summer home in the mountains of Western North Carolina the place now called "High Hampton" when he received his nomination for Governor on the Democratic ticket. He went to Columbia immediately, after he had accepted the nomination, he went from county to county as the Democratic Committees arranged for him to speak to assembled crowds of citizens. The men wearing red shirts were always there, standing quietly by.

In the Pickens Sentinel July 10, 1876: "The citizens of Pickens Court House and vicinity are respectfully invited to meet in the grove facing the Griffin house near the public spring tomorrow morning at eight o'clock for the purpose of clearing off the grounds for a successful Democratic meeting Tuesday, July 15th when Gen. Wade Hampton and other noted speakers will be here. Seats will be built and we hope to obtain a band. Dinner will be served for the guest speakers in private homes." (1958 location of Sentinel).

Some of the first settlers of Pickens have told their children and grand-children of that exciting day. The Democratic Clubs from all of the eight Townships came riding into town wearing their red shirts, there were several hundred of them. A band had been obtained from Greenville. The town officers kept a sharp watch for illicit liquor peddlers, and only a few drunks were arrested that day. The speeches were long and interesting to those who were deeply concerned in the State's politics. Even the local Republicans had a deep regard for Gen. Wade Hampton and his plans for redeeming the State.

Tension in politics grew as time for the November election day approached. At all County seats, and other places where trouble was expected a detachment of United States soldiers was stationed. Each poll had three managers—two Republican and one Democrat. Men wearing red shirts stood close by and saw that no negroes were forced to vote the Republican ticket. Most of the United States Troops stood by and allowed the Democrats to vote unheeded, as long as there were no violent disputes. The election in Pickens

County was almost unanimous for Hampton and there was little trouble.

Tension increased after the election The returns came in slowly and it was evident from the first to the election Board of Canvassers at Columbia that the Democrats had elected the Governor, Lieutenant Governor, Secretary of State, Attorney General, and Comptroller General The Republicans had elected the State Treasurer, State Superintendent of Education, and Adjutant and Inspector General. The Republicans had a majority of 1100 for Presidential electors. The Democrats had elected two out of five Congressmen, and five out of eight Solicitors. Seats in the House of Representatives were given to sixty-four Democrats and sixty Republicans. The State Senate had twelve Democrats and six Republicans. Since the hold-over Senators numbered twelve Republicans and three Democrats, it gave the Democrats a majority of one in the Legislature. But the outcome was not settled. The Republicans claimed fraud in the election and Chamberlain did everything in his power to hinder the Democrats. After the Supreme Court had declared the election valid Chamberlain had certificates of election printed for all of the Legislators except those from Laurens and Edgefield Counties, by this action giving the majority of seats to the Republicans.

The night before the Legislature was to convene Chamberlain ordered soldiers marched into the State House and stationed on the second floor in the wide hall between the State Chamber and the Hall of the House of Representatives. The soldiers were ordered to keep out all persons who did not have the right credentials.

The next day, Nov. 28, 1876, was one of the most critical days in the history of South Carolina. If the outraged Democrats had vented their wrath the State House would have been red with blood. A great crowd of Democrats from all parts of South Carolina was in the Plaza in front of the Capitol. Chamberlain sat in the Governor's office and watched them through the windows.

When Gen. Hampton suddenly came before them they grew quiet. In a calm voice he told them to keep peace: "It is of the greatest importance to us all as citizens of South Carolina that peace should be preserved. I appeal to all of you white men, and colored men, as Carolinians to use every effort to keep down violence. — I beg all of you, my friends, to disperse and leave the grounds of the State House, and I advise all the negroes to do the same—We trsut the Law and Constitution and we have perfect faith in the justness of our Cause."

Many Pickens County people of a past generation believed that Gen. Wade Hampton prevented the beginning of another Civil War. Chamberlain tried for several weeks, and by various schemes to hold the Governor's office but Gen. Wade Hampton finally got the place he had won.

At the same time these squabbles were taking place in our State Government Samuel Tilden, Democrat, and Rutherford B. Hayes, Republican, were having a dispute over the Presidential election. Hayes finally won.

In April 1877 Governor Hampton went on a mission to Washington to appeal to the new President to remove the United States Troops from South Carolina. His appeal was granted and on April 10, 1877 the last of the Troops marched out of Columbia, South Carolina, thus ringing down the curtain on the Reconstruction period. There were other problems to be solved and other mistakes to be righted but the citizens of the "Prostrate State" began to see the light.

The Hon. Armistead Burt, a distinguished jurist of Abbeville, addressed the Spring term of Court in Pickens in 1877. He said it was the first all white jury he had addressed in a long time.

An item in the Sentinel about that time said: "It has

been announced that from five to seven thousand negroes have recently left Edgefield and Laurens Counties on their way to Arkansas."

In spite of the troubles of Reconstruction the new **Pickens County** had continued to progress and carry on. Announced in the Sentinel:

"A fair number of schools are open in the county, and the only hindrance seems to be that the appropriation is too small to support them for the length of time they should run."

J. H. Carlisle was Superintendent of a school in Pickens that was called a "boarding school." Many of the students came from isolated sections of the county and boarded in homes for six to ten dollars a month. The classes were taught in the first little log school house near the present food locker.

The school was run in two terms. The first term began January 12th and ended May 20th. The second term began June 20th and ended November 13th. The following courses of study were given:

"Primary Department, Junior Class: 1st Term, Webster's Spelling; Reading, Seargant's Series.

"2nd Term: Spelling and Reading continued; Primary Geography, Mental Arithmetic, Exercises in Writing.

"Intermediate Class: 1st Term: Georgraphy, Reading and Writing continued; Elements of Written Arithmetic, Introductory English Grammar.

"2nd Term Intermediate: Geography completed. Elements of Written Arithmetic completed. Analytical English Grammar; Primary United States History Exercises in Writing.

"Junior Class 1st Term: Latin Grammar Latin Reader; Elementary Algebra completed; Natural Philosophy.

"Intermediate Preparatory Department 1st Term: Six

105

Books of Virgil Greek Reader completed; Kendrick's Greek; Higher Composition and Rhetoric; Plain Geometry.

"2nd Term: Advanced lessons in Greek, Higher Algebra, New Universal Solid and Spherical Geometry (Chemistry.

"Senior Class, 1st Term: Cicero's Select Orations; Trigonometry; Roman History; Latin Prose Composition."

These classes will prepare candidates for Sophomore Class in college.

The tuition terms of this school were: Primary and Juniors $5 per student; Intermediate $10; and Seniors $12.50. Special preparation was $20. Some of the young law students of the town assisted Mr. Carlisle in teaching this school. Among them were the late Hon. James P. Carey, Sr., the late Hon. Julius E. Boggs, Sr., and the late Judge T. J. Mauldin.

Mr. C. L. Hollingsworth, a prominent attorney, had built a large two-story frame house on the corner facing Main Street near the schoolhouse and the young men read law under his supervision when they were not holding classes.

Easley had a school that was supervised by J. Q. Stockman, a noted preacher and teacher, with about the same curriculum as the one in Pickens. W. K. Boggs was teaching at Liberty, and R. L. Lewis was the School Superintendent at Central.

At that time each Township was considered a School District. In 1875 the following School Trustees were elected for the eight School Districts at a meeting held in the Court House; by the School Commissioner and Board of Examiners: "1st District, Pickensville, R. E. Holcombe, R. E. Bowen, and J. R. Gossett; 2nd District, Salubrity, Laban Mauldin, M. T. Smith, and Thomas Parkins; 3rd District (Garvin (Central). E. H. Lawrence, J. N. Arnold, and James P. Hendricks; 5th District, Pickens C. H., W. T. McFall,

H. J. Anthony, and W. B. Allgood. 6th District, Dacusville:
B. F. Morgan, W. T. Field, and M. L. Jones. 7th District:
Pumpkintown, Van S. Jones, Gideon Lynch, and M. Gillespie 8th District: Eastatoe, Col. William Nimmons, T. J.
Lewis, and Thomas N. McKinney.

Items from Easley for the Sentinel stated: "The Easley
Baptist Church, one of the first fruits of the Baptist Mission
Board on the Airline Railroad has started a Sunday School.
And the Methodist Church states they have done likewise.

"Business is good and several new homes are going up.
The well diggers are kept busy, and home owners are setting
out trees and flowers.

"Clyde and Mote are running the 'Easley Hotel' which
is near the depot. Mr. Clyde has established a hack line to
Pickens, which he runs when the roads are not too muddy.
In summer he furnishes transportation to the scenic Caesar's
Head and Table Rock Hotels. Ox wagons haul merchandise
to Pickens in bad weather.

"New Baptist Churches have been established at George's
Creek on the east side of Pickens County, and one at Prater's
Creek in the Pea Ridge section. These churches drew members from older churches that were farther away. And each
community is increasing in population, from the natural
growth of families, and from new citizens who are moving
in. The beauty of Pickens County with its mountain scenery,
its good farm lands and water power, and its healthful climate
is attracting many people."

As early as 1873 the Editor of the Pickens Sentinel received a letter from the Art Editor of Scribner's Magazine
inquiring about Table Rock mountain, "That I may come
and take pictures of the same."

We wonder if the picture of our Table Rock ever appeared in Scribner's Magazine.

The young people of Pickens County wanted fun and

entertainment in those days as much as they do now, but they were easier pleased. It did not take as much excitement to amuse them. There were no moving pictures, no radioes or T V, and a girl had to be engaged to a boy before she could go buggy riding with him. But they managed a good deal of courting and every once in a while there was a big wedding in somebody's home. Church weddings were practically unknown until the 1890's.

After the marriage there was always a big supper for everybody, and dancing for the young people. Usually somebody played a fiddle or picked a banjo, or played a mouth organ. The square dance, or the Virginia Reel was their favorite form of dancing. Nobody went on a trip then but every bride had a wedding dress and a "second-day" dress. The second day was called the "in-fair" and consisted of another big dinner and another dance at the groom's home.

Neighbors often got together to help each other work in the rural areas and when the work was done this furnished another occasion for feasting and singing or dancing.

Favorite entertainments among the young people in town were corn poppings and candy pullings in winter, and cake walks or debates on humorous subjects. In summer young boys went to the swimming hole in the pasture but a girl would have been disgraced if she had put on a bathing suit. No swimming for her.

Sorghum Molasses was used for a candy pulling and the plates and hands were greased with butter. Depending on the number of guests a large or small kettle of molasses was put on the stove to cook. By that time every kitchen proudly bore an "Iron King" cook stove. If the kitchen was large several couples could pull candy at the same time. When the molasses had boiled sufficiently it was poured into the buttered plates to cool; and when it was cool enough to handle a boy took one end of it and his partner the other and slung it back and forth to each other until it had made a yellow rope. If they pulled long enough it turned almost white. And after it was too hard to pull they broke it up in pieces and sat around the open fire talking while they ate it. This was winter fun.

The Cake-walks were performed by the couples arranging themselves for a Grand March around the room, the first couple holding a short cane in front of them. After the march started when they reached a certain place in the room the hostess blew a whistle and the cane was passed to the next couple, rapidly. The girls and boys were having fun marching with their sweethearts and when a pistol was fired the couple that had the cane got the cake, which was usually a big pound cake. And then they danced a while and cut the cake for refreshments.

There were protracted meetings at almost every church in the county at some time during the summer. It was a good place to renew old friendships and sometimes make new friends and many a courtship started from some young couple holding a song book together. If they lived in the country the family all rode in the wagon together to meeting and when the long sermon and the song service was over they all rode home together again.

As time went on a few of the more successful young farmers acquired top buggies, and some of the family men bought surreys with fringe around the top—like town folks, but there was a wide difference then. Everybody accepted life as it came without jumping into the future.

The Pickens County Musical and Sunday School Convention met at Griffin Baptist Church in September 1876. It enrolled the names of more than one hundred permanent members.

The roads of the County were often in bad shape. An item appeared in the Sentinel in July, 1876: "The public roads are in a very bad condition. Now that the farmers are done 'laying by' we hope the Road Commissioners will give them work restoring the roads."

Another item of interest in the newspaper stated: "Mr. J. W. Brown has exhibited several samples of what appears to be valuable iron ore. He says it crops out on the side of Sassafras Mountain. We have also been informed that a rich lead mine exists in that section, from which slugs were taken years ago by the earliest settlers and the Indians, and molded into bullets for fire-arms." But so far as we know it was never investigated. The item in the paper stated further that when the Sassafras Gap Railroad went that way it would probably be discovered. But the railroad was never built.

In the 1850's, and even after the Civil War there were attempts at goldmining. Many times along in the 1870's and 1880's the wealth of mica, soapstone, and other minerals were exploited by ambitious citizens to no avail. Along in the 1930's there seemed to be a prospect of oil, but that too fell through. In 1957-1958 there was a county-wide search for beauxite without avail.

Chapter XI

The talk of a "Sassafras Gap" Railroad which was in the newspapers from 1873 to 1876 changed in the late 1870's to what was called the "Eastatoe Gap" Railroad. A clipping from a Greenville News of Sept. 16, 1879 says: "The citizens of Transylvania, N. C. held a mass meeting at Brevard today in the interest of the Belton, Williamston, and Easley Railroad which is to pass through the Blue Ridge Mountains at Eastatoe Gap and go down the French Broad Valley by way of Brevard to Asheville. Representatives were there from Buncombe and Henderson Counties North Carolina and from Pickens and Anderson Counties, South Carolina.

Col. R. E. Bowen of Pickens County was called upon to address the meeting. He told of his previous efforts and failure to obtain a charter from the South Carolina Legislature for a narrow gage road through Sassafras Gap, and of the subsequent passage of the charter for the present road. He also told of the fortunate discovery of Wm. T. Kirk (Chief Engineer) of the Eastatoe Gap. He assured his audience that South Carolina intended to build the road to the State line and expected North Carolina to take it from there. He believed the road was now an accomplished prospect.

Maj. Thomas B. Lee (Engineer) who had assisted Capt. Kirk in making the survey gave his report: "We found a smooth and continuous ridge from Belton to Easley (25 miles) which can be graded at small cost. There are several streams to cross between Easley and the mountains, which will cause some heavy work. From the foot of the mountains to the top of the Blue Ridge at Eastatoe Gap the work is heavy and expensive, but accessible at all times. The curvature is large but may not exceed 578 which is easily passed by locomotives and not uncommon on railroads.

Major Lee continued with the figures of his survey all the way to Asheville, and the audience seemed greatly impressed. But the railroad was never built on account of a lack of subscriptions.

About this time the county was besieged by peddlers coming through with stolen goods. No doubt the cloth was stolen because they sold it for two cents to ten cents a yard. But there was a catch in it for they always brought along suits of clothes and ladies dresses or coats that were priced extremely high, for which they would take money or good country produce, such as hams or corn and wheat.

On October 12, 1883 a newspaper called "The Easley Messenger" started publication in Easley, with A. W. Hudgens and J. R. Hagood as Editors. The slogan for the paper was, "Truth, like a torch, the more it's shook, it shines."

There were many advertisements in the Easley Messenger: "The Dry Goods Emporium, Dr. J. W. Quillian, Easley, S. C., also Drugs and Medicines.; Furniture House, A. M. Runion; A New Lot of Ladies' Hats, Ribbons, and Laces. Robinson and Wyatt, Dry Goods. W. M. Hagood & Co., General Merchandise; Hudgen & Hudgens Cotton Buyers, and Dealers in General Merchandise." As time went on there were many others.

The Church Directory gave: "Baptist Church, Rev. J. W. Hutchins every first Sunday at eleven A.M. Sunday School every Sabbath at 3:30 P.M. The late Rev. D. W. Hiott was their second pastor.

Methodist Church:—Rev. S. P. H. Elwell, Pastor— every fourth Sabbath at eleven AM; and 7:30 P.M. Every second Sabbath at 7:30 PM by Rev. D. R. Brown. Sunday School at 9:30 AM every Sabbath.

The Postmaster General advertised for applicants to carry mail over the following scheduled routes from July 1st 1884 to June 30, 1888. Contracts to be duly executed before May 17, 1884.

"No. 14105 From Pickens C.H. by Anderson's Mills and Baker, to Nine Times, 13 miles and back three times a week. (Bond $600).

No. 14106 From Pickens C.H. by Redmond, Crow Creek, Mile Creek, and Eastatoe to Fall Creek 22 miles and back, twice a week, Bond $400.

No. 14107 From Pickens C.H. by Flower, Prater's, and Six Mile, to Stewart 20 miles and back twice a week. (Bond $400).

No. 14108 From Easley by 18 Mile, Major's, and Hickory Flat to Pendleton 18 miles and back, twice a week (Bond $400)

No. 14109 From Easley by Rice's to Pickens C.H. 8½ miles and back six times a week. (Bond $500.)

No. 14110 From Easley to Briggs and Dacusville to Table Mountain, returning by way of Maynard to Easley, 15 miles and back, three times a week, (Bond $500).

No. 14111 From Sunny Dale by Knob and Rock to Wattaco, 15 miles and back, once a week, (Bond $200).

Mr. Alonzo M. Folger had moved from Pickens to Easley and was at this time the Postmaster there.

A new store in Easley "Owensby Brothers" had a full page advertisement for Christmas goods.

Easley had built a new school which they called the "Academy." It was a two-story frame building over on the north side of town near the old Higgins place. Prof. Moore was Principal of the school at that time and he was an active leader among the young people, doing many things to see that they were inspired and entertained. And during his administration in those early years of the 1880's there were many entertainments, plays, and pageants put on by the young people of Easley under his guidance.

The trustees of this school in 1883 were: Elias Day,

A. W. Hudgens, Isaac Williams, W. M. Hagood, J. R. Gossett, J. A. Higgins, and W. W. Robinson, Sr.

Original Assessment of Personal Property in Pickens County 1883—Auditor's figures:

"1166 horses	$ 57,291.00
1146 mules	65,693.00
4236 cattle	45,122.00
2411 Sheep	2,416.00
8330 Hogs	16,516.00
1218 Dogs	1,490.00
216 watches & silver	3,546.00
94 pianos, organs	4,032.00
1572 carriages & wagons	32,966.00
Average value merchandise	33,150.00
Materials pertaining to manufacture	586.00
Average value machinery, engines, tools	24,176.00
Money on hand including Bank Bills & etc.	9,423.00
Value of all Credits	27,585.00
Stocks	60.00
Bonds	1,125.00
Other property	73,643.00
Total for the year 1883	$398,821.00
Total for 1882	352,409.00
Gain over 1883	46,412.00

The figures fixed by the Supply bill for Pickens County are 18 mills. Eight for interest and Railroad Bonds. (Remember the $100,000 assumed for Railroads Bonds when the Air Line was built.)

In February 1884 the School Law was amended to allow the School Commissioner, with the consent of the Board of Examiners, to appropriate from the two mill tax on property a sum not to exceed $200 to defray the expenses of the Teachers' Institute.

In the early 1880's a school had been built in Pickens that was often called a college. It was known as "The Piedmont Institute." It stood on the west end of Main Street on a hill, a big frame Victorian building. Before this building was erected the School Commission and his Board had secured Prof. William M. McCaslan and his cultured wife to open a school in the McFall building which stood on the corner where the South Carolina National Bank now stands (1958). James McFall, one of the first merchants in Pickens had built a store and dwelling combined on that corner when he first came to Pickens. His wife was a daughter of Dr. John Robinson. It was a rather large building and now it was turned into an auditorium and school rooms. (Mr James McFall had died in 1875 and his brother, Waddy T McFall, bought his stock of goods from the widow and moved it into his own building across the street where the Gulf Filling Station 1958 stands. (He ran a large general store there for many years.) He died 1904.

Easley had just built its new "Academy" and after seeing the splendid school work the McCaslans were doing they made Prof. McCaslan a good offer that almost pulled him away from Pickens, but the Pickens people got busy and went in debt for the large new school building which they called "The Piedmont Institute."

Soon a real educational system was enjoyed in Pickens by the local young people and those from the neighboring towns, and other students who came from as far away as Georgia and North Carolina. Prof. McCaslan kept adding to the curriculum and employing extra teachers as the student body grew. Prof. McCaslan had charge of the Latin and Greek classes. Mrs. McCaslan, Miss Eliza Aiken, and Miss LaRue taught literary subjects, and Prof. Black taught Mathematics. Miss Nannie Edwards of Due West taught music, and Miss Carrie McMakin who bore the distinction of having organized the first childrens' chorus in Spartanburg taught voice and elocution

115

In the August 15, 1884 issue of the Easley Messenger, we read:

"On Saturday night of last week it was our good fortune to enjoy a musical and literary treat at the Piedmont Institute in Pickens. Some of the finest talent of Pickens Couny and our neighboring city of Greenville favored us with strains of sweet music, and their inspiring presence.

"The exercises opened with the music of a string band, and then the following program was enjoyed:

1. "The Mocking Bird' splendidly executed by Messrs Alexander, Barr, and Bruce, with Miss Lucy V. Hagood at the piano.

2. Songs and chorus. 'Wait Till the Clouds Roll By'. Sung by Misses Byrd and Hillhouse of Greenville, Miss Maggie Simpson of Pendleton, Miss Nina Lewis of Pickens; and Mr. Walter Barr, and P. McD. Alexander of Pickens.

3. "A play—1776-1876—given by young people of Pendleton and Pickens.

4. Several instrumental duets.

5. Solo—'Annie Laurie' by Miss Byrd of Greenville.

6. Song—'I'se Gwine Back to Dixie.' Quartet with Miss Hagood at the piano."

"The encore was loud and long and they responded with: "Never Take the Horseshoe From the Door."

"An instrumental hymn, "In the Sweet Bye and Bye" was played by the string band, in closing.

The Piedmont Institute was a wonderful school while it lasted. It acquired a great deal of prestige and prominence but the debt for the building was too great for the small town and it was placed on the block five or six years after it was built.

The place was bought by the Hon. James P. Carey, Sr., who had married Miss Linda Lovett who came from Georgia to attend school. They did some remodeling and turned it into a home. Their children grew up there. After the passing of Mr. and Mrs. Carey the building was torn down and the lots on the front became business property.

For a time Pickens was without a schoolhouse and classes were held in any vacant building, and in the Masonic Hall. Then a single story building was erected where Mrs. Ernest Folger's home stands on Main Street. (1958)

The Official Census of 1880 showed that Pickens County had the smallest population of any county in South Carolina, numbering 14,391, with 7,149 males, and 7,242 females. Charleston County had the largest population and Spartanburg County the second largest.

An item in the Sentinel December 2, 1880 is headed, "An observation on Railroad Taxes." It tries to emphasize that every question has two sides and that the people who are still grumbling about the tax on the original Railroad Bonds should consider what the railroad has meant to Pickens County by increasing the market value of farm produce and by the tax it pays the County.

In October 1881 Commissioner of Agriculture, A. P. Butler, sent notices to the Granges in every county to urge their cooperation in sending farm exhibits to the "Cotton Exposition" in Atlanta. Some of his remarks were: "At the last regular session of the Legislature an Act was passed creating an Agricultural Department. We will soon have display cases in our rooms in Columbia for exhibits of produce from every county in the state. They will be carefully arranged in the proper cases and plainly marked with the name of the County and the contributor."

Advertisement of Bibles appeared in every paper. "As many as 50,000 small Bibles will be printed each day until the demand is met. The New Testament Complete for 10 cents. The Gospels complete for 7 cents. The Gospels separately, each 2 cents. Larger Bibles complete, Morroco, gilt edges for $1.50."

A Minister's and Deacons' meeting was held at Mountain Grove Church on May 28th, 1881. The following men were present: Ministers—D. C. Freeman, Benjamin Holder, T. W. Tolleson, J. C. Parrott, G. M. Lynch, M. L. Jones, G. W. Simmons, J. T. Burdine, Jahes M. Stewart, and J. T. Lewis.

The Deacons were: Jacob Lewis, T. P. Looper, J. A. Griffin, H. J. Lewis, O. P. Fields, N. B. Edens, C. D. Stephens, R. A. Baker, A. B. Chastain, F. C. Parsons, J. M. Porter, William Aiken, C. P. Barrett, C. Durham, and WM. Bryson."

The Presbyterian Church in Pickens was in process of being organized from 1878 until 1882 when the first public worship was held in the partly finished frame church on the same location where the brick church stands 1958. In the spring of 1878 a petition had been signed by Presbyterians in the village and surrounding country asking for a Presbyterian Church in Pickens. Prior to the organization of their church the Presbyterians had worshipped in the Methodist Church, with visiting minsters since 1871, and in the Baptist Church at Secona.

The Charter Members of the Pickens Presbyterian Church were: "Mrs. Zealy Ann Ambler, Julius E. Boggs, Sr., Mrs. Emma Bruce, Clarence A. Bruce, James McDuffie Bruce, Miss Minnie Lee Bruce, Mrs. Julia A. Folger, Dr. George W. Earle, Mrs. Jeannette Earle, Mrs. Malinda A. Hollingsworth, C. L. Hollingsworth, and Mrs. Minnie McFall." Mrs. Emma Ambler Gilreath was received into the Church on profession of faith, was baptised by the Rev. R. H. Nall and accepted as a Charter Member. C. L. Hollingsworth gave the land for the Church and Cemetery. The women of the church helped to raise the $600 that it took to put up the first frame building. At first the Church formed a group with Carmel and Mt. Pleasant, near Easley, promising to pay $160 of the $700 Salary for pastoral services of the Rev. A. P. Nicholson for one fourth of his time. A Sunday School was organized in 1882.

Dr. Riley became pastor of the church in 1883 and continued to serve it for sixteen years. C. L. Hollingsworth, and Julius E. Boggs, Sr., were elected, ordained, and installed elders, and Dr. G. W. Earle, deacon.

The Easley Presbyterian Church was organized on May 9th, 1886 in t he Easley Academy, the Rev. McL. Seabrook officiating. There were seventeen Charter Members; W. M. Hagood, Thomas A. Archer. Mrs, T. A. Archer, J. McD. Bruce, Dr. J. W. Earle, W. W. Ford, Mrs. W. W. Ford, C. T. Martin, Essie Russell (Folger), Dr. R. J. Gilliland, Sr., Mrs. R. J. Gilliland, Dr. Joe B. George, Mrs. Bright Gilstrap, W. A. Mauldin, Mrs. W. A. Mauldin, Mrs. Alice Russell, Mrs. John G. Wyatt.

The pastor of the new church was the Rev. John Riley. The officers elected and installed were: W. W. Ford and C. T. Martin elders; W. A. Mauldin and J. McD. Bruce as deacons.' (J. McD. Bruce had moved his residence to Easley for a time, but later came back to Pickens where he spent the rest of his life).

The original church building of the Easley Presbyterian Church was erected in 1887 on Church Street at its present location on land donated by W. M. Hagood, Sr. The session met for the first time in the church Feb. 12th, 1888. C. T. Martin resigned as Clerk of the Session and W. M. Hagood, Sr., was elected and held the office for many years.

An item in the Easley Messenger said: "Easley is really getting on a boom. Five new families have recently moved to town to educate their children."

The first wedding in the Presbyterian Church in Pickens was in the nature of a double wedding, although the couples were married by separate clergymen. The contracting parties were from two of the best known families in Pickens at that time.

The account of the wedding in the Sentinel says: "The marriage of Prof. Henry Harris of Staunton, Virginia, and Miss Addie Hollingsworth, daughter of Capt. C. L. Hollingsworth; and Hon. J. E. Boggs, a member of the Legislature, and Miss Minnie Bruce took place in the Presbyterian Church in Pickens on Sunday the 24th of December 1882.

"The church was crowded at the appointed hour when the three officiating clergymen came down the center aisle together. The two visiting pastors were accompanied by Rev. A. P. Nicholson who was serving the church as pastor at that time. Then, down the aisle came Mr. Harris of Virginia, brother of one groom and Miss Gould of Charleston; second Mr. Harris of Texas and Miss Calhoun of Ninety-Six, and third came Prof. Henry Harris and Miss Addie Hollingsworth. They took their places on one side and waited until the second couple and their attendants had arrived, down the other aisle. First, Mr. McD. Bruce and Mr. John L. Hollingsworth, then Mr. G. W. Taylor and Miss Lucie Hagood of Charleston, and after them Hon. J. E. Boggs and Miss Minnie Bruce.

"When the two parties were in place at the front of the church the Rev. Dr. Darby of Columbia stepped forward and in a very impressive ceremony united in marriage Prof. Harris and Miss Hollingsworth. Then the Rev. Mr. Grogan of Georgia came forward and in a solemn and beautiful ceremony united Mr. Boggs and Miss Bruce. At the conclusion of both ceremonies the young couples took their seats and by invitation of the pastor of the church Dr. Darby entered the pulpit and preacehd a magnificent sermon. Prof. Harris and his bride left for their home in Virginia the next day."

On December the 22, 1884 J. R. Hagood the young Editor of the "Easley Messenger" died with a sudden attack of influenza and diptheria. He was a graduate of Wofford

120

College and only 23 years old. His very successful newspaper had been running a little more than a year when he died. An item in the "Messenger" January 2, 1885 states:

"For the present Mr. J. P. Carey of Pickens will assume control of the editorial department of the paper and Mr. W. M. Hagood of Easley will manage the business portion."

The Messenger continued to run for a while and then there was another Easley newspaper called "The Easley Democrat." with Mr. D. F. Bradley, editor.

After Gen. Wade Hampton was elected Governor of South Carolina 1876 he served almost two full terms. In 1879 he was elected to the United States Senate and the Lieutenant Governor, W. D. Simpson, of Laurens, took his place. But in 1880 Gov. Simpson was made Chief Justice of the State, and Thomas B. Jeeter, president of the State Senate became Governor, temporarily.

The Presidential election was on in 1880, as well as election for State officers. James A. Garfield was elected President of the United States on the Republican ticket.

Johnson Hagood was running for Governor of South Carolina and won the election, although some allegations of fraud were claimed. The census of 1880 showed a considerable increase in population in Pickens County.

In 1881 a stock law was passed in South Carolina that required people to fence their pastures and keep livestock on their own premises. Several humorous incidents occurred and some controversy over this new law.

An item appeared in the Sentinel 1882, headed Liberty: —for some time past our Council has been trying to enforce the stock law, and the ordinance imposes a fine of one dollar for animals found running loose.

"A few days ago one of our neighbors unfortunately left his gate open, the cow walked out and he had to appear before the mayor with one dollar. About the same time another cow had strayed into town from the outskirts and her owner had to come forth with his dollar. Before the laughs had subsided one of the Councilmen saw his little Jersey Bull "Pack" come walking down the street and that gave the town three dollars. It looked like money making business when Mr. S. Robertson appeared with a rope, looking for his calf that had strayed."

At the January term of Court 1884 in Pickens the Grand Jury gave the following presentment: "We the Grand Jury respectfully submit our report: "We have examined the offices and records of all County offices and find them in good condition and neatly kept.

"We have visited the Poor Farm and find the paupers are properly cared for and the farm in good condition. We have visited the jail and find that the jailer is doing his duty.

"We recommend that the walls of the jail be repainted on the lower floor and whitewashed on the second floor.

"We further recommend that the County Commissioners sell such portions of real estate in town that belong to the County and apply the amount to remodeling the Court House, which was hastily constructed in the beginning. And we do recommend that the Court House be enlarged so as to meet the necessities and wants of the Court at the earliest time possible. And to put up more shelving in the Clerk of Court's Office to take better care of records.

"We further recommend that the well at the rear of the Court House be cleaned out frequently and kept in sanitary condition, and we feel there is a great need for a privy to be erected on the back of the Court House Square for the convenience of the public."

Several cases were presented for the attention of the Court. Most of them were liquor cases, or trouble that had come by the illicit selling or drinking of corn liquor. There were three or four bar-rooms in town, and drunks were frequently on the streets.

Pickens was a country village then with a well at each end of the wide sandy Main Street, a livery stable for hiring horses, buggies and hacks stood near the east end of the street a little past the stores. Several oak trees, very large and perhaps very old graced the center of Main Street from the location of the present First Baptist Church to the Presbyterian Church. Chickens and ducks and geese were often seen on the Court House Square, for most of the residences were close in. On the west end of Main Street Hagood and Alexander had a general merchandise store, facing the W. T. McFall store across the street, and beyond the McFall store Mr. W. H. Ashmore had a Blacksmith Shop for many years. Then there was a residence or two.

In 1882 Hugh S. Thompson was elected Governor of South Carolina. He had served as State Superintendent of Education for several terms and was a very able man. The State continued prosperous during his administration and several cotton mills came South. He was reelected for a second term but resigned in July 1886 to accept the appointment of Assistant Secretary of the United States Treasury, and Lieutenant Governor Sheppard became Governor of South Carolina, for the rest of the term.

On August 31, 1886 before midnight the State of South Carolina was racked by a terrific earthquake. Many buildings in Charleston were demolished, and even Pickens County in this far corner of the State was shocked and frightened by chimneys fallings and dishes jumping out of cabinets. It was new and strange, almost a phenomenon to country people who had heard little about earthquakes. They dreaded its return for years, but it never came.

And speaking of phenomenon, there was an occurrence in Pickens County about that time that has been handed down as a traditioal story for generations, by reliable citizens. The names have not been changed. Mr. D. F. Bradley was Editor of the Pickens Sentinel for many years. His father, Mr. Joel Bradley, was an old man who lived alone on what was then called "Mauldin's Mountain" (later "Byars' Mountain") between Easley and Liberty. Old Mr. Bradley had been sick for a long time with a negro man nursing him. He finally died and some of the white men in the community went to sit with the corpse that night. There were no funeral homes at that time, and no embalmers. The neighbors and friends did what they could. The relatives stayed until bedtime and went home, and the two men, Elias Mauldin and William Smith, stayed for the night. And this was their version of the story: "It was a hot summer night with stars shining dimly, but no moon. It was stifling in the room where the corpse lay in a simple homemade casket. There was only the light of a single candle. Their story:

"We went out on the little porch to get a breath of fresh air and as we sat we saw, at a little distance from the house, what looked like two balls of fire, as large as grape fruit, rise up and seemingly chase each other. At first we thought it was two people coming with lanterns. But the things wove in and out, sometimes high, sometimes low and all the time they were coming nearer the house. Finally, one of them passed the house and the other came directly beside us and went in the open door.

"We sprang up as it passed us and stood paralyzed watching. It circled the room and went out the open window and that was the last we saw of them. We couldn't leave the body alone and neither of us was willing for the other to go for help. No need of help anyway, but daylight has never been so welcome."

This is not a ghost story, nor intended as such. It actually happened in Pickens County seventy-five years ago. It was a strange weird experience that was never explained. Whether the queer balls of light were the so-called "fox fire", or some strange form of gas no one could say. But the fact remains that similar balls of light have been seen on Brown Mountain in the Smokies of North Carolina from time immemorial, and scientists and geoligists have searched in vain for some explanation of them.

Chapter 11

In an old newspaper (The Pendleton Messenger 1825) when boat travel was the mode of the day, an article appeared about a party of men who came to Pendleton from Columbia and went by boat up the Seneca and Keowee Rivers, and Cane Creek to MR. WHITMIRE'S PLACE.

In a Pickens Sentinel dated 1896 (71 years later) this article appeared:

"Eighteen miles northwest of Pickens in the beautiful valley of Cane Creek is the hospitable home of Silas Hinkle. It was settled a hundred years ago (1796) by Dicky Whitmire and Silas Hinkle's father bought it from his estate.

"The dwelling nestles beneath the outstretched arms of magnificent shade trees where the hills recedes and the valley expends into a wide fertile bottom. Forty yards north of the house runs the creek, cold and clear. In the side of the granite wall of the creek a spring house has been hewn out of the rock. It is enclosed by a wooden door shutter, and just below it is the spring across a gangway from the house."

Before the day of phonographs, radio, and TV there were many fiddles and banjos in the country. Most of them were crude and homemade but a few had been brought from the "old country" by some music loving ancestor. Those were real treasures and furnished a pattern by which a clever workman could copy himself one.

There seemed to be a real musician in almost every community, and always enough talent to play for parties and square dances. Some of the old slave-time negroes were real musicians on the fiddle and banjo.

Along in the late 1890's and early 1900's singing

schools were frequently held at the country churches in summer, and a singing teacher always came from some larger town to teach the people how to read notes and harmonize.

Mr. Jim Parsons of Liberty was a talented fiddler in his day. He played without benefit of music lessons and won distinction at several "Fiddlers' Conventions" he attended in Atlanta and Asheville.

Chapter 12

On October 21, 1886 there was an announcement in the Pickens Sentinel: "A mass meeting of the Pickens County Agricultural Society will be held in the Pickens Court House the next Sale Day. All farmers are invited to come and take part in the 'Farmers' Movement' which has caused a great deal of gas and smoke, but seems to be getting into shape to make itself felt in the Legislature in the near future. Come everybody!"

We are told in a later issue of the paper that the meeting was well attended and that four delegates from Pickens County attended the Farmers' Convention in Columbia: C. L. Hollingsworth, W. T. Field, J. H. Bowen, and W. T. O'Dell."

The Granges seemed to be giving place to what was known as the "Farmer's Alliance."

At the Convention in Columbia resolutions were adopted stating that in the year 1862, Congress had appropriated certain land scrip, the proceeds of the sale of which should be a fund, the interest of which should be used to sustain an agricultural and mechanical college, for the education of the industrial classes in each State accepting the donation; that South Carolina had accepted the fund, but had failed, under the stress of War, to carry out the conditions. The Legislature was urged to estabish a real agricultural and mechanical college, and that the control of that college be given to the Board of Agriculture. And that experimental stations be established at such college to be under the control of its faculty, and that Congress be asked to pass the Hatch Bill appropriating $15,000 annually to each State for this purpose, and that the Congressmen and Senators from this State be urged to work for its passage. The Convention further stated that such an appropraition was not to be received by the trustees of the South Carolina College as its Agricultural Annex was inadequate.

At this same time Thomas G. Clemson, an old man then, often sat dreaming of an Agricultural School at his home, Fort Hill, S. C., and when he died in 1888 he left the complete plans for such a school in his will. But his desires did not come to pass immediately on account of a family law-suit, and might never have been entirely successful without the untiring efforts of Benjamin R. Tillman. John Peter Richardson, who was Governor of South Carolina for two terms 1886-1890, seemed slow to act in favor of South Carolina accepting the legacy of $80,000 and around 800 acres of land for an agricultural school. A part of the Clemson acreage is in Pickens County.

Agriculture and Education seemed to be the leading questions of the day in Pickens County in the 1880's and 1890's, as elsewhere in South Carolina. This State had always had a few good schools on the pay as you go plan. The so called "free schools" that existed before the Civil War were free only to the parents who were unable to educate their children, or to orphans. Free schools usually ran a shorter term, and were quite unlike our "public schools" of today. In 1850 there were 56,000 children of elementary school age in South Carolina, and 17,838 of them were in "free" schools.

There have been school changes at intervals through the years. In 1850 a Board of seven Free School Commissioners was appointed by the General Assembly for a term of three years. The constitution of 1868 provided for a County School Commissioner elected bienally by the electors of the County. He was ex-offcio a member of the State Board of Education; and a member of the County Board of teacher examiners, to which until 1885, he appointed the other two members. The general school law of 1896 replaced the County School Commissioner and the County Board of Examiners with the County Superintendent of Education and a Board of Education. Mr. J. K. Riley was the first Superintendent of Education in Pickens County, 1896-1899.

In July 1889 this item appeared in the Pickens County newspapers: "I have been requested by the Adjutant General of the United States Army to nominate a candidate from the 3rd Congressional District for appointment to the Military Academy at West Point for examination not later than the 14th of June 1890; whose appointment is required to be made as nearly as one year in advance as possible.

"A competitive examination will be held at Abbeville Court House, S. C. on Friday July 21, next, beginning at 10 o'clock A.M."—Further requirements for the examination were stated and the article was signed, J. S. Cothran, M.C. 3rd Congresscional District of South Carolina."

Frank G. Mauldin, the eldest son of Joab Mauldin and his wife Deborah Hollingsworth, stood the examination and got the appointment. He made the Army his career and attained the rank of Brigadier General before he retired. He was the first man from Pickens County to attend West Point.

All of the papers were full of the work that was going on at Clemson, for at last it was an established fact that this section was soon to have an Agricultural College. There was much sawing of timber and hauling on the grounds where the Main Building was going up. The building that was to become "Tillman Hall." Several big barns and silos were built for housing the stock and ensilage. Around sixty mules were kept for hauling, and a herd of dairy cattle to furnish milk for the workmen, many of whom were State convicts.

On June 2, 1890 a murder occured in Pickens on the sidewalk in front of the present (1958) Ford automobile agency. Mr. Stephens lived in a house that stood near there and Mr. Griffin, the man who was killed, lived with his mother at the big white house, the Griffin place. At that time there were no other houses on Ann Street. The newspaper states: "Last Saturday the first murder was committed in the town of Pickens. David S. Stephens stabbed John C. Girffin in the left breast, inflicting a mortal wound from which Mr. Griffin died in about two hours."

It was a lengthy story about a quarrel over a sawmill that the two men owned, and that Stephens had been operating at Clemson. They happened to meet in the Post-office just after Griffin had returned from Clemson and walked down the street toward their homes arguing. There were several witnesses who testified that Stephens stabbed Griffin and fled as soon as he saw him fall. He has never been heard from since. Domestic trouble was involved.

Quoting the Sentinel again: "The Sheriff hastily rounded up a posse of men and searched for Stephens all night, without avail.

"*Three hundred postal cards* were printed the next day giving an account of the murder and an accurate description of Stephens, and offering a $500 reward for his arrest. These were mailed to all parts of North Carolina, where he was supposed to have gone, but he was never arrested."

There were no telephones then, and no automobiles for quick travel. It was almost a day's journey on horseback or in a buggy to the foot of the mountains. And there was no F.B.I. It was almost impossible to apprehend escaped criminals. Out of sight was soon out of mind.

The negroes in Pickens County had small schools and churches in all of the towns, and some in the rural areas. Their Baptist Church was established in Pickens in 1886. Mingo Young, Peter Hagood, Israel Ferguson, the McKinneys, Sizemores, McDonalds, Allgoods and others of a past generation were faithful members. Cold Springs, Soapstone, Nebo, and Shoal Creek were some of their rural Baptist Churches. Their Methodist church in Pickens was established in the 1890's and they had rural Methodist churches.

Union and Crossroads (west of Pickens), and others in each town.

Mr. J. E. Boggs had become the Editor of the Pickens Sentinel. Another paper "The People's Journal" had been established by Mr. T. C. Robinson in Pickens, two weekly newspapers in a very small town. "The Easley Democrat" was still running in Easley, where Mr. D. F. Bradley had moved to become its editor.

A Pickens County Interdenominational Sunday School Convention was organized at Liberty in the summer of 1889. The following Township Presidents were elected: Pickens, J. E. Boggs; Easley, A. W. Hudgens; Liberty, S. G. Sterling; Central, B. J. Johnson; Hurricane, L. R. Dalton; Eastatoe, Rev. John T. Lewis; Pumpkintown, Matthew Hendricks; Dacusville, Rev. J. E. Foster.

After much discussion and many recommendations and financial arrangements the corner stone of a new Court House was laid in Pickens 1890. The newspaper account of it says: "Last Saturday the corner stone of a new Court House was laid in Pickens with the solemn and impressive ceremonies of the Masonic Order by Keowee Lodge No. 79 A.F.M., J. E. Boggs W.M.

"Owing to the short notice given no extensive preparations had been made. Everything went off in a smooth and quiet way. The following articles were placed in the receptacle: "Letter Head of J. T. Boggs, Liberty; Harris and Morris, Pickens; $20 Continental bill, Sept. 26, 1878. Rev. Ben Holder; roll of officers and members of Bates Lodge A.F.M. Easley; Postal card of J. H. Brown, Liberty; card of Capt. Elias Day, Contractor; issue of Sentinel containing write up of Clemson College; letter from the Editor of the Setinel to the Editor that may be present at the opening; Copies of News and Courier, Sept. 12th, Anderson Intelligencer, Sept. 17, Keowee Courier, August 26, names of Sentinel force; Greenville News Sept. 26, Easley Democrat Sept. 25 copy of the State Sept. 24th; names of the Sheriff's family: Mr. and Mrs. H. A. Richey, Flora, Dora, Cora, Homer, Nora, Olga, Sadie, James, and Ola; $100 J. E. Hagood; three copies People's Journal; $50 Confederate bill by Jerre Looper; fifty cents Confederate, J. E. Hagood."

Abandoned lands were sold by the Sheriff of Pickens County under the Act of December 24th, 1889:

unknown—8017 acres at 18 cents per acre; Estate of E. Gilstrap, 790 acres at 15 cents per acre, 450 acres at 20 cents per acre, 6110 acres at 19 cents per acre. All of this bought by J. E. Hagood. 1800 acres at 17 cents per acre bought by B. F. Perry, Greenville.

The town of Calhoun (lately changed to Clemson) was established on the Air Line Railroad in 1892. It is near Clemson College and has always served as the railroad depot for that institution. It is Four miles west of the town of Central.

Mr. B. J. Motz was the first depot agent and used an empty box car for his office until the depot was built.

Mr. W. H. Hester built a neat and commodious store room and Mr. Jesse Payne ran the first store. Other small businesses started. James Dillard, John Fennell, and J. W. Cochran built homes. Two old settled places were near the little town, The old Keowee Heights which had burned was near there, the John T. Carey place and the J. W. Craw-ford home. A State road was soon built to the college and the Ft. Hill Postoffice was there for a while. Other homes and stores were built as time passed.

Several cotton mills had been built in South Carolina but none in Pickens County until 1895 when the Norris Cotton mill was established. A notice of the organizational meeting of this mill appeared in the People's Journal April 11, 1895:

"The following group of men met in Dr. L. G. Clay-ton's office at Central. D. K. Norris, T. M. Norris, A. B.

Williams, H. C. Shirley, F. L. Garvin, J. F. Hendricks, T. L. Watkins, G. M. Norris, T. C. Martin, J. F. Lay, T. C. Robinson, W. V. Clayton, E. B. Richardson, B. P. Kelly, James Hall, Hovey Smith, J. M. Hook, W. L. McGee, Hugh McCarter, and L. G. Clayton.

"D. K. Norris stated the object of the meeting, read the notice of the call and the commission of the corporators. D. K. Norris was elected chairman of the meeting and L. G. Clayton, Secretary.

"On motion, it was ordered that the notice of the call and the commission of the corporators be accepted as information.

"The chairman read the subscription list 676 shares which the stockholders present held, or represented, and which amounted to $67,600. This was received as information and the chairman declared that it was competent under the law for the stockholders to organize a company for purposes stated in the commission. The proposed by-laws were read ·y J. P. Smith.

"The election of Directors of the Company was then held by ballot, and the following gentlemen were elected: T. L. Connor, D. K. Norris, G. M. Norris, J. H. Dozier, J. F. Lay, J. P. Smith, and W. V. Clayton.

"D. K. Norris was elected president of the Company.

"A tentative location had been selected where the water ran over some shoals on Twelve Mile River about four miles from Central and five miles from Liberty, and a little more than a mile from the main line of the railroad. An engineer was employed to survey the proposed location of the plant, which was to run by water power."

The location was found to be satisfactory and the cotton mill was built on a flat beside the river with the main entrance of the mill from the top down. This proved to be satisfactory for general purposes, but inconvenient for handling heavy machinery and other necessities. Some years after the mill was built when the late Mr. O. L. Craig was cotton buyer and outside overseer, he devised a plan for building a service road through the woods to the base of the mill. The Board approved his plan and he did the first grading with a tractor from his farm. The road proved beneficial in many ways. It provided extra parking space for workers at the base of the mill, and a more convenient means of loading and unloading heavy necessities. It continues to function as a monument to Mr. Craig's ingenuity. In 1958 paved roads lead to and from Cateechee.

The Postoffice at the Norris Cotton Mill was named "Cateechee" and a picturesque village grew up around the mill. The houses and yards are well kept, there is a good elementary school, and a beautiful Union Church where all denominations worship together. And in 1957 they have several progressive clubs among the women and an attractive community house. The management has changed where death has taken its toll.

The Norris Mill management built a freight depot and warehouse at the railroad about a mile from the mill and the town "Norris" grew up around that. There was already a one room school near the place, known as "Johnston's Chapel" and it soon became the Norris school. A church and homes were built.

At intervals through the years the size of the little school grew to fit the increasing population until the citizens of Norris were able to build an up-to-date brick schoolhouse.

Among the educators who have served as Principals there: Miss Mary Grice, Noah Hendricks, Miss Maggie Lewis, Miss Myrtie Boroughs, Dr. Joel Bowen, John O. Hicks, W. T. Earle, R. T. Hallum, W. E. Dendy, Mr. Petree, L. E. Kirby, Miss E. Wilson, Col Joe M. Robertson, W. E. Myers, S. E. Burnett, W. F. Welborn, and C. C. Boroughs.

Notes from the Hurricane District of Pickens County

in 1889: "Stewart Postoffice: A good portion of our township is known as Pea Ridge but it is opening up fast. Crops are good and the spirit of improvement is abroad in the land. Some of our miller friends have added flouring departments. Uncle Johnnie Stewart recently caught the spirit of progress and added a gin to his old moss-covered mill on Six Mile Creek, which would be the delight of an artist. The old sawmills are giving way to first class circular saws.

"Prater's Creek has a neat, comfortable church building. The old Boroughs Mill is still turning and their store is a good place to swap tall tales.

"Elijah Brown has opened a store at "One Mile" and T. Finley one above that. They intend building a church at Four Mile soon."

And on the other side of the County Dacusville reported: "J. O. Davis has one of the best schools in the county with a daily average of 31 pupils a day for ten months. Looper Bros. are building a large and commodious store at Looper's gin. Crops are good and people are working hard.

July 3rd, 1889 was appointed by the State Superintendent of Education as the time for competitive examinations for girls who were seeking appointments to the new Winthrop Training School then in connection with the South Carolina College at Columbia. The successful applicant will receive the State apointment, equivalent to $150 per session of nine months. We checked at Winthrop and found no Pickens County girl's name on the first list—a few years later, after the school moved to Rock Hill there were many.

The question of prohibition was the main issue in every election campaign in South Carolina in the late 1880's, and local option was still harassing the church people when Benjamin R. Tillman became Governor in 1890. Almost every term of court in Pickens County had a number of liquor cases, or cases that had been caused by the liquor traffic. Tillman was an outspoken Governor whose sympathy was always with the masses. He knew that several open bar-rooms in every town was bad for the general population and he advocated a Dispensary Law. It would prohibit the sale of liquor except by the State. One liquor store to be placed in each County seat, with no drinking on the premises, and the liquor to be sold in sealed packages of pints, quarts, or gallons. A vote was taken at the election of 1892 to test the people on the question of prohibition. Though the majority of the best people favored it the total vote was a minority of the white vote of the State. When the Legislature met the Dispensary Law was passed as a compromise, with the profits from the sale of liquor to go to school funds. The law went into operation July 1, 1893, during Tillman's second term as Governor, but it was attended with trouble from the first. It was declared unconstitutional by the Supreme Court in April 1894 and its operation was suspended until August of that year when a new Court sustained the law. The Dispensary in Pickens County was located at Pickens, the court house town. There was still a great deal of wrangling over the Dispensary in various parts of the State.

John Gary Evans was elected Governor of South Carolina in 1894, and Benjamin R. Tillman was elected United States Senator.

There was a financial panic in 1893 and the price of cotton and other farm products were at their lowest ebb. Cotton was around five cents a pound, corn fifty cents a bushel, chickens fifteen cents each, regardless of size, beef and pork eight or ten cents a pound.

W. H. Ellerbe was elected Governor in 1896 and died during his second term of office in 1899, and the Lieutenant Governor M. B. McSweeney became Governor. After he had served out Ellerbe's unexpired term McSweeney was elected for a full term. The main issue of the election was still the Dispensary and Prohibition. He was for the Dispensary.

The War with Spain came on in 1898 and every county

in South Carolina responded when called on. The late I. M. Mauldin, was Captain of a company that went from Pickens.

Cuba had long desired independence from Spain and had engaged in several unsuccessful revolutions but in 1897 when the Spanish soldiers drove the Cuban farmers into the cities to starve to death the United States became indignant and sent the battleship "Maine" to Havana Harbor to protect American interests in Cuba. The ship was blown up and its crew was killed which immediately brought on the Spanish-American War.

Owing to the increased expenditures of the United States government on account of the War, industry began to revive all over the country. Gold had been discovered in Alaska about that time and owing to the annual increase of gold much of it was coined into gold money. Around 1900 more than five million dollars was invested in cotton mills in South Carolina. At Easley, in Pickens County, Mr. W. M. Hagood, Sr., became president of Glenwood Mill and Mr. John M. Geer was elected president of the "Easley" Mill, both new.

Easley was expanding rapidly. There were many new homes and stores, but along in the 1890's they had a disastrous fire. A report of this appeared in the Greenville News: "Our neighbor town of Easley had four bnildings destroyed in a recent fire. The fire broke out in the office of the "Easley Democrat." It was said to have started from a defective stove flu. Nobody was in the office at the time and the fire was well under way before it was discovered. Easley having no fire department nor city water supply the citizens formed a bucket brigade.

"Inspite of all efforts the flames spread rapidly. A one story frame house beyond the printing office soon caught and a two-story frame store building owned by W. M. Hagood and used as a furniture and coffin store was the next to go. By that time the fire was so fierce that the bucket brigade had no effect on it and they devoted their efforts to saving other buildings by keeping them as wet as possible, and removing what goods and furnishings they could. The two story brick building of Hagood & Company next to the furniture store, used as a general store and occupied by the bank was the next to go. Many of the goods had been taken from that. The vault and safe of the bank remained safe. The losses were estimated at around $18,600 not covered by in-surance." Soon there was a report in the papers that Easley had four new brick stores built by Jameson brothers.

At about that time there was a great deal of talk and planning to make Pickens County a summer resort.

The following notices appeared in the papers: "At Easley there are three hotels besides private boarding houses, at which the best of accomodations may be had. There is also a livery stable where rigs may be obtained to visit the magnificent surrounding country.

"At Liberty there are also good boarding houses and livery stable accomodations, and as hospitable people as anyone could hope to find.

"Central, as its name implies, is the midway point between Atlanta and Charlotte. The railroad furnishes one of the best eating places on the whole Air Line railroad, and there are also private boarding places and livery accomodations to drive to the beautiful Twelve Mile and Keowee country, where the streams are full of fish.

"Pickens Court House is near the center of the County, and nearer the beautiful Blue Ridge Mountains. It also has transporttaion and good drivers to take you for a meal at the noted Ambler House, to Alexander's in Eastatoe, or even to the hotel at Table Rock if you plan to be on a two or three day trip in the mountains. The Thornley House is a splendid hotel in Pickens. Summer residents are beginning to build houses here. Mr. B. A. Hagood of Charleston has just completed a large summer home. (This the White Hotel 1958).

139

(Minutes First Baptist Church): "The Pickens Baptist Church was constituted May 16, 1891 in the Presbyterian Church at Pickens Court House. Dr. Manly preached an able sermon after which the constitution and organization took place. Dr. T. M. Bailey was elected Moderator, and Rev. J. M. Stewart, Secretary. Other members of the Council were: Rev. W. B. Singleton, Rev. J. T. Lewis, Rev. Charles Manly, and Rev. T. F. Nelson

Letters of dismission from other churches were read and twenty-nine members were enrolled.

After forming the Constitution and articles of faith in Christ for a church in Pickens a motion was made, and adopted, that the church be named "The Pickens Baptist Church."

At a later meeting the committee submitted offers of suitable locations for the church, some lots were for sale, others as gifts. It was finally decided to accept the lot offered for a church by Rev. J. M. Stewart on west Main Street. It was a year or two later before the small white frame church was erected, and many years later the new church was built at the present loction.

From the time Pickens was established in 1868 the Baptists had worshipped at Secona, or Griffin neighboring Baptist churches, or they had been given the opportunity by the Methodists and Presbyterians to invite Baptist pastors and hold services in their churches. It had created a nice order of fellowship among them, and the other denominations had enjoyed hearing their visiting pastors.

Chapter 13

In 1900 Pickens County proudly boasted: "Two railroads, (Southern and Pickens Railroad), three cotton mills (Easley, Glenwood, and Norris Mill), two banks one in Easley, one in Pickens, three roller mills, thirty-seven saw mills, ten shingle mills, and four brick yards. There were churches in every part of the County, Methodist, Baptist, and Presbyterian. There were no other denominations at that time. Schools were getting more numerous, although many of them were small and housed in very crude buildings. And the effort to have graded schools was still depending on a larger State appropriation.

For several years after the dream of a Sassafras Gap Railroad, and the one from Augusta to Chicago, known as the "Eastatoe Gap" Railroad had fallen through, the leading men of Pickens County worked faithfnlly to establish a Short Line Railroad from Easley to Pickens.

An Act was approved by the Legislature December 24, 1890 that constituted the following men as a body politic and corporate by the name of the "Pickens Railroad Company": S. D. Stewart, J. D. Smith, J. P. Carey, M. W. Newton, W. R. Price, J. K. Kirksey, J. M. Stewart, and J. E. Boggs.

The capital stock of this company was thirty-five thousand dollars, "with the privilege of increasing the capital stock to such amount as may be found necessary, not to exceed one million dollars."

It was decided by the County Commissioners to hold an election at the voting precinct in each Township and submit to the qualified voters the question of subscribing in seven per cent coupon bonds of said respective Township. The

County Commissioners fixed the amounts of the following Townships: Pickens, C. H., $10,000; Eastatoe Township, $3500, Hurricane Township $3500, as requested by their respective petitions on file in the Court House.

The following managers were appointed for their respective precincts: Pickens, C. H., J. E. Hagood, Jr.; Ludd Hawthorne, and J. B. Freeman—Eastatoe Township, J. W. Thomas, A. A. Alexander, and Robert W. Gilstrap; Hurricane Township, Six Mile Precinct, W. H. Thomas, Aaron Garrett, and J. S. Barker; Prater's, J. E. Boroughs, W. N. Bolding, and W. L. Morgan; Mile Creek: L. R. Dalton, J. E. Parsons, and J. S. Bowen.

The above amounts were subscribed and also $300 from Easley. This was in 1891. There were many more meetings and other subscriptions before the railroad was completed in 1898.

At a Directors meeting in 1892 the following officers of the proposed railroad were elected: J. E. Boggs, President; J. H. Burkhalter (Construction Manager) Vice-President; T. D. Harris was elected Secretary and Treasurer, and J. P. Carey, Attorney. But later T. D. Harris resigned and Mr. Caery served as Secretary and Treasurer.

When the Pickens Railroad was finished in 1898 Capt. John T. Taylor, conductor and maanger of the road, and Mr. W. T. (Bill) Jeanes, the engineer offered the people a free ride. The train had one passenger coach and two or three freight cars. A few men and several small boys accepted the ride. In after years when one of the small boys had grown to manhood he liked to tell of that ride, and the wreck that was frightening but caused no serious damage.

"The whistle blew and we were on our way", he said. "We sank back on the shiny red plush seats which seemed the height of luxury to us. We had never ridden a train before, but we were extremely confident of this strange new vehicle. Suddenly it slid off the rails and went bumping along on the cross-ties for several yards. That was very exciting to small boys and we laughed boisterously until we saw the men were getting frightened, and then suddenly the coach turned over on its side, and we felt doomed. We were a badly bruised and frightened bunch of little boys when the train men came to pull us out, but fortunately nobody was seriously hurt."

The Heath, Bruce, Morrow store came to Pickens in the early 1900's. Local citizens called it "the Big Store." It was the biggest store built in Pickens until the 1958 Winn-Dixie. It covered the space now occupied by the Sinclair Filling Station, the cafe and Duke Power Co. It carried a general line of merchandise and millinery, with a "hat trimmer" from Atlanta each season. Women doted on hats in those days. Some of them bought "Merry Widow" sailors as big as cart wheels.

The late T. L. Bivens, Sr., who became a very influential citizen of Pickens County moved here with his wife and family about the time the Big Store came. Mrs. Bivens, before her marriage, was Miss Daisy Heath of Charlotte, N. C.

Pickens and Easley cooperated well in their use of the new short line railroad. One newspaper item in 1900 said: "The Pickens brick machines are turning out 50,000 brick a day and many of them are going to Easley over the new railroad to supply the brick structures that are being built in that town. Already, the Directors of the railroad have had to buy more freight cars."

A little brcik building was erected for the first bank in Pickens. It afterwards became "Lovell's Shoe Shop." It was named "The Pickens Bank" but changed to "The South Carolina National" many years later, after the present building had been erected, for the South Carolina National.

W. T. McFall helped organize, and served as president of the first "Pickens Bank," and J. McD. Bruce was Cashier. After it became the South Carolina National Bank the sons of the first two men continued to work in the bank together, Frank McFall and J. Hagood Bruce, assisted by J. E. Boggs, Jr., who later became Manager until his death when D. Clyde Garrett became Manager until 1958.

In 1900 Main Street in Pickens was wide and dusty, or muddy, depending on the weather. There was a well at each end of the street and big oak trees that soon gave way to progress. The livery stable, at the east end of Main Street had perked up a bit with some trotting horses and rubber tired buggies for the young sports who couldn't afford to own a rig.

Other stores were, Folger, Thornley & Company, at the old Hagood-Bruce stand, Hendricks Brothers, W. T. McFall (across the street), Harvey Richey, T. D. Harris, and A. M. Morris in the first brick store, built in Pickens (1896.) A Jew named Louis Copel had a store in that block, and farther down street was the Masonic Hall and Craig Brothers Store. There were trees along the sidewalks in front of the stores that soon gave way to progress. But the wells at each end of Main Street stayed until actual street work began. W. T. McFall died in 1905 and his store became Moore, Mauldin & Co. for a few years, and then a gas station.

Almost every Saturday a patent medicine barker was on the Court House Square telling the people about the newest wonder medicine and offering free prizes with every bottle. A big crowd always gathered around him as he told of wonderful cures that had been made. After his speech about the medicine he would hold up a flashy ring, and say: "Get a gold ring free, a ring set with topazes from the running rivers of Alaska." And the men and women would give their hard-earned cotton money for a ring and a bottle of medicine. Perhaps the word "Alaska" had intrigued them for only a few years past several Pickens County men had gone to Alaska while the gold rush of the 90's was on.

Sometimes there was preaching on the Court House Square, and sometimes a wedding to the delight of the spectators. A blind man and his wife often sat in front of the stores on Saturday singing and picking a guitar, with a tin cup in evidence for free-will offerings. Teams and wagons passed along the street loaded with country produce and often there were several members of a family sitting in chairs in the back of a wagon. An occasional top buggy passed, or a new rubber-tired open buggy with a dressed up driver and a sleek looking horse. Those were "the good old days," before automobiles.

The first Pickens High School was built in 1904.

The Pickens Cotton Mill was built in 1906. A charter was applied for May 4, 1906 by the following petitioners: W. M. Hagood, Sr., John M. Geer, W. C. Smith, James P. Carey, Sr., J. McD. Bruce, R. E. Bruce (not related), and F. W. Poe. The mill was organized with 137 stockholders. The first stockholder's meeting was held in the Pickens Court House June 15, 1906. Three presidents have served the Pickens Mill since 1906: W. M. Hagood, Sr., 1906-1925; his son, C. B. Hagood 1925-1933; Ben F. Hagood, Sr., 1933.

Sixty houses were built at the Pickens Mill in the beginning and others have been built as needed. The first school was taught in a four room mill cottage with the partitions removed. On Sundays the same cottage was used for church purposes. Mr. John Edens was the first school teacher, and the Rev. Seabrook Atkinson was the first pastor. Capt. J. T. Taylor, conductor of the Pickens Railroad, and an active member of the First Baptist Church in Pickens, organized the first Sunday School at the Pickens Mill.

The coming of cotton mills to our section increased the cotton acreage in Pickens County. In the early 1900's all of the creek and river bottoms were planted in corn and the upland was in cotton. Most of the farmers had patches of wheat, oats, sorghum, and they usually grew enough fruit and vegetables for home use; and hogs, cows, and chickens which they fed from the surplus produce around the farm. It was a great day when they had found the many uses of cotton seed instead of dumping them into the creeks as their ancestors had done. And then oil mills were built.

There were many good country homes in Pickens County where descendants of early settlers lived along the Keowee, Saluda, and Oolenoy Rivers, and in the section around Six Mile Mountain. The small towns were largely made up of the sons and daughters of these, with a sprinkle of newcomers from other sections. And at times some of the sons and daughters moved to Greenville, Atlanta, and other distant points.

Many families in the mountains who had long been trained in the art of spinning and weaving moved to the cotton mills to earn a regular salary instead of depending on uncertain crops. And the lure of schools also drew them. People, as a whole, were becoming more conscious of the need of an education for their children. The school buildings scattered throughout the country were poorly heated and unsanitary, and often children had to walk four or five miles to school. The older boys and girls were growing ambitious for higher deucation and each year more boys went to Clemson, Furman, and Wofford, and the girls to Winthrop, Lander, and G.W.C. (now a part of Furman), or Chicora at Greenville, or Converse at Spartanburg. Some of their parents were financially able to send them and some went by scholarships, or by working their way through.

Some of the tenant farmers continued to live on cotton farms as long as the production of cotton kept up and their children trudged back and forth to the old field schools until the State gave better support and fairly comfortable schools were built in every community, or school buses transported them to town.

The negro population which was never large in Pickens County, and which is the smallest in South Carolina in 1958 has a few good farmers but the largest percentage are in public works. Their schools and churches have kept pace with the times, according to State regulations.

The Dispensary profits which went to the school system at first, amounted to $175,000 in 1900. In 1903 the amount had dropped to $126,000 which showed that the sale of liquor through legal channels had fallen off. In 1902 half of the profit was given to the road fund, and half to the town in which the Dispensary was located.

The Dispensary continued to cause trouble in many parts of the State where it had been unwelcome in the beginning. Charges of fraud were often made against the Government Distilleries that supplied the Dispensarys. They all closed in 1906 and only the bootleggers remained.

EASLEY

In the early part of 1900 Easley was getting new schools and churches established for its two mill villages. The Easley Progress started publication in 1902 with C. T. Martin as editor. The "Southern" bought the main line railroad and had ambitious plans of double tracking it from Atlanta to Charlotte.

There was a great deal of talk of moving the railroad away from the Main Street of Easley and building a depot near the present overhead bridge on the Easley-Pickens highway, but the merchants were opposed to the change and the double track went through the center of the town. A new hotel and new homes and stores were being built. A few of the first old houses remained. An old Briggs house with beds of clove pinks and other old-fashioned flowers was near the first home of the Easley Progress. Farther down the street, still standing (1958) was the first W. W. Robinson house (a Confederate soldier who married Miss Elvira Hagood, a daughter of the Caesar's Head Benjamin Hagood.) Their son, W. W. Robinson who married Miss Sallie Payne was one of Easley's leading merchants for many years, grandfather of the present generation of Robinsons.

W. M. Hagood, Sr., W. C. Smith and Clarence Folger were the first bankers in Easley. Dr. R. F. Smith of Slabtown, who married Miss Ida Hollingsworth, daughter of C. L. Hollingsworth of Pickens, was the first doctor in Easley. And Dr. Jim Gilliland, Dr. Earl Russel and Dr. Charles Wyatt came soon afterward. A Dr. Folger from North Carolina practiced at Pickensville long after Dr. John Robinson had moved to Greenville and passed away.

About the time that W. M. Hagood, Sr., became president of Glenwood Mill he sold his mercantile business to W. W. Robinson and a Mr. Thornton and for many years that was the largest dry-goods store in Easley. Mr. Ed Robinson and others had grocery stores. Miss Lillian Sholar ran a small millinery shop for more than a decade. Mr. N. D. Taylor was the first town photographer, and Mr. Harvey Snyder was the first jeweler. There were numerous other stores and shops.

About 1906 a traveling library was organized in Easley by Miss Haveline Thompkins, Librarian of the Neblett Free Library. Each case that was sent out contained fifty books and the collection embraced books of fiction, history, farming, cooking, hygiene, travel and miscellaneous. Something for every taste. The Southern Railroad furnished free transportation and any community could get a case of books by writing an application to the Neblett Free Library, and having it signed by three reliable citizens.

The first case sent out from Easley went to the home of Mr. John W. Rosamond at Brushy Creek, with Miss Jenny Rosamond as community Librarian.

A cotton gin and oil mill with a railroad sidetrack was built in the early 1900's where it stands in 1958.

A large brick high school building was erected in Easley in 1904 on the corner where the Easley Postoffice stands 1958, but farther back from the street. After the new high school was built several years later it became the Lanier Manufacturing Company's place of business.

LIBERTY

Liberty applied for a new charter in 1900 and set up a regular city government with a Mayor and council. Mr. W. O. Willard, if not the first, was one of the earliest Mayors. Others who have served since 1900 are, C. H. Perkins, J. F. Bannister, C. E. Bush, H. M. Chapman, E. J. Bryson, C. C. Lewis, J. D. Black and John Callaham.

Liberty had an Oil Mill and Cotton Gin before 1900. Its first bank, one of the first brick buildings in town, was opened for business in 1901 with J. Carter, president, W. T. O'Dell, vice-president, and H. C. Shirley, Cashier. The Farmer's and Merchant's Bank was organized 1909 with W. H. Chapman, president; T. J. Mauldin, vice-president; and H. M. Chapman, Cashier.

In the early 1900's there was a Callaham general store at Liberty, Junius Boggs had a dry-goods store, Mr. John Rankin a hardware, feed, and grocery combined, and Mr. Tom Hunter and a Mr. Robinson were partners in a general store. Mr. McCord had a meat market, and a colored man ran a barber shop. There was a small frame Post Office.

In 1901 Mr. Jeptha P. Smith organized and started the first Cotton Mill, which he called the Liberty Mill. In 1904 Mr. Lang Clayton started another mill and called it the Calumet Mill, at first. Later it was called "Maplecroft." The two men were presidents of their respective mills.

149

In a few years Mr. John Geer, president of the Easley Mill bought the two Liberty mills and called them Easley Mills Two and Three. In 1920, after Mr. Geer's death, the Woodside interests bought the mills and they are now called "Woodside Mills two and three."

Both mills have exceptionally nice Baptist churches. The Calumet Church was organized 1910. The first church organized at the other mill, now called Woodside number two, was a union chnurch, but it changed to Baptist in 1915 and is called the "East Side Baptist Church." It has a large, well equipped brick building, with a new educational building.

The Presbyterian Church in Liberty was the off-spring of the old Carmel Presbyterian Church. Many of its members had ancestors who had worshipped at Carmel in days gone by. The first frame building was erected in 1883, the present brick building in 1913. Mr. E. R. Horton, a Baptist friend, subscribed the first fifty dollars toward a Presbyterian church in Liberty.

The First Baptist Church in Liberty, instituted between 1780-90 is mentioned with other very old churches in another section.

The Liberty Methodist Church was built at its present location about 1907.

Liberty's schools have progressed steadily from the first log schoolhouse at Salubrity to the present well equipped High School and Elementary School buildings, and athletic grounds.

Sidewalks, electric lights, and an up-to-date water system were installed in Liberty in the early years of 1900, with street paving and lighting and added water facilities as the years passed.

The Six Mile Community had wanted a good school for a long time. They felt that their prayers had been answered when the Baptist Academy came to them in 1910. Before that their schools had been few and far between. The older generation had made an appeal to the Twelve Mile Baptist Association as early as 1876 for some means of giving their children a Christian education. The Association had gone on record favoring such a school, but nothing came of it publicly for a long time. Many prayers had been spoken before it finally came to pass.

In 1909 the Twelve Mile Association appealed to the Home Mission Board for help, and this time the appeal met with immediate response. The school was built within the next year and opened for students in October 1910.

It became the pride and joy of the Six Mile Community when a throng of boys and girls entered its halls, eager to begin this new experience. There was an Administration Building with class rooms. A girls' dormitory and a boys' dormitory.

Mr. V. E. Rector was the first Superintendent assisted by Miss Cecil Hester, Mr. P. M. Durham, and Mr. McDuff Weams in charge of the music program. Superintendents who succeeded Mr. Rector were, Mr. J. E. Grimm, Mr. S. E. Garner, Mr. J. E. Willis.

The school closed about ten years after it started, for lack of adequate funds to keep it going, but the Six Mile Community will always be grateful for the time it spent in their midst.

It was a God given opportunity for many isolated young people and gave them the incentive for a broader way of life.

CENTRAL

Central had grown into a prosperous town, with cultural advantages at home and at Clemson College nearby. It had a good school, Methodist, Baptist, and Presbyterian churches. The Farmer's Bank was a live institution. It had the usual number of stores and small shops, and cotton gins.

And then the "Southern" bought the railroad and there were many changes. Almost immediately the railroad shops moved to Greenville, and some of the workmen moved with them. The big Railroad Dining Room closed and many people were looking for work. Some grew discouraged and moved away after the town had two or three disastrous fires. Among the first builders of the town who remained to help it build back were the Claytons, Morgans, Gaines, Gassaway, Rowland, Hall, Brock, Folger, Werner, Shirley, Eaton, Smith, Carson, Brown, Kelly, Beardon, and others.

The leading men knew that the town must have an industry of some kind to bring back its former prosperity. Cotton mills were the order of the day, and with the help and guidance of Col. D. K. Norris they established the Isaqueena Cotton Mill of 25,680 spindles which brought a good pay roll. Col. Norris was elected president of the mill and held that offcie until his death when Mr. R. G. Gaines was elected president. In a few years Mr. Gaines resigned on account of bad health and his half brother, Mr. W. L. Gassaway of Greenville became president.

Wesleyan Methodism was organized in South Carolina in 1893. At the annual Conference in 1901 a committee was named to secure a suitable place for a school to aid in this work, the committee to serve as a Board of Trustees for such a school. They were to raise funds, construct buildings, hire teachers and put the school in operation. By 1903 there was a strong feeling that the school when founded should be a connectional institution, and the conference so voted.

The Rev. Eber Teter, Connectional Missionary Secretary called a meeting of the Presidents of the Wesleyan Methodist Southern Conference. At that meeting the present site was selected, in Central, S. C.

Funds not being available in the Educational Society it was agreed that the Missionary Society proceed with the building of a school until the Educational Society was prepared to take full charge. Charles B. Smith gave the site for the school.

Smith Hall, the Administration Building was erected in 1906. In 1907 a privately owned girls' dormitory was completed, to be managed by Rev. A. C. Dunwoody and his wife. In 1908 Teter Hall for boys was opened.

Rev. L. J. Harrington of the Illinois Conference became the first president, with his wife, Nellie L. Harrington, as preceptress. Mr. and Mrs. James Hancock, who attended school the first year, were assistant teachers. The school opened for its first term on October 15, 1906, with an enrollment of nineteen. The number increased to sixty-three before the end of the first school year. In 1909 the school became Wesleyan Methodist College and was authorized to grant B.A., B.S., and Bachelor of Divinity Degrees.

On April 4, 1928 the local Board of Managers met in the college auditorium with special representatives of the Connectional Board to reorganize the work of the school. As a result, the college department was reduced to junior rating, except for the four years of theological training.

The junior college department has had consistent growth since that time. Its present student body includes students from fourteen states and one foreign country.

In 1953 the Junior College Department was fully accredited by the Southern Association of Colleges and Secondary Schools, and the University of South Carolina agreed to accept full transcript from the Junior College. In 1955 the Bible College was accredited by the Accrediting Association of Bible Institutes and Bible Colleges.

"The purpose of Wesleyan Methodist Junior College, restated to fit the enlarged curriculum offering, was to provide for the people of its constituency the opportunity for two years of college training in the liberal arts and sciences, in a Christian atmosphere.

"The influence which Wesleyan Methodist College has exerted over the lives of students throughout its history cannot be measured. No doubt it has been one of the great factors in developing the work of Wesleyan Methodism in the South."

PICKENS

The Carey Building was erected in Pickens and in 1909 the Keowee Bank opened for business in the same quarters that in 1958 became the new "Pickens Bank." Mr. James P. Carey, Sr., was president. The Keowee Drug Store was opened by Dr. Earle E. Lewis.

The first Pickens County Fair was held in Pickens in the Fall of 1909, and it was so successful that another was held in the Fall of 1910, but bad weather dampened the ardor that time and it was 1923 before another Fair was held at the County seat. Easley had a Community Fair, and then Central took over for the County for several years before it went back to Easley again, with a Fair and horse show at Pope Field.

Coleman L. Blease was elected Governor of South Carolina in 1910. He was a dramatic stump speaker, tall, handsome, with a heavy black moustache. He always wore a black stetson hat and would throw it over the heads of the crowd to impress them when he was striving to put some point across. After he was elected he almost cleared out the penitentiary pardoning men, some who had been sent in for life. Several Pickens County criminals were among these.

Political speakings drew big crowds in those days, whether it was men running for local, State, or National offices, everybody went.

In 1911 Grace Methodist Church, a beautiful brick structure, was built in Pickens. The little white church among the pines, which had been the first church built in the County seat, and which had served the people well for forty years was sold to the Wesleyan Methodists and moved down the Easley highway to become "Pickens View" Church. Several miles west of Pickens "Mountain View" Baptist Church had been established in 1909.

In 1914 Hon. T. J. Mauldin resigned as State Senator from Pickens County to become Judge of the newly created 13th Judicial Circuit.

Judge Mauldin was the son of Joab Mauldin (firs. sheriff of Pickens County) and his wife Deborah Reed Hollingsworth. He was born on the farm of his parents near Pickens July 21, 1870. He received his primary education in Pickens and entered the Citadel at Charleston in 1887, the first beneficiary student from Pickens County. After completing the four year course at the Citadel with honors he taught school for two years. He was Principal of the last private school in Laurens before the establishment of the public school system in the State.

He studied law at the office of his uncle C. L. Hollingsworth in Pickens, assisting him with minor cases for practice. He was admitted to the Bar in December 1892. The Pickens Sentinel had changed its name to the Sentinel Journal, and as a side-line Mr. Mauldin became editor of the paper. In 1904 he was elected to the Legislature and served one term, not offering for reelection. In 1910 he was elected Senator from Pickens County. He served one full term and it was during the last year of his second term that his appointment to the judgeship came.

He married Miss Frances Miles Hagood of Charleston,

and Pickens, Sept. 28, 1904. They had no children. Judge Mauldin died October 22, 1931 at his home in Pickens.

Mrs. Mauldin is fondly remembered by many friends in Pickens County as "Miss Queen." She was a great club woman and a great humanitarian. She died Feb. 26, 1954.

Chapter 14

A great local flood came down the Keowee River in the summer of 1916 when the Toxaway Dam broke and released a tremendous volume of water. The Toxaway Dam was a massive structure of dirt and field stones built to impound the waters of Lake Sapphire at a resort hotel in Western North Carolina. A rainy summer had caused seepage in the dam and it broke about seven o'clock on the evening of August 13th. Runners were sent out to warn the citizens in its path and word passed from house to house down the valleys "Leave your homes and seek higher ground."

The people did that and only four or five lives were lost, but several mountain homes were damaged beyond repair, and some of the smaller cabins were submerged or completely washed away. At one place the roof had to be taken off the barn to let the horses swim out. Huge trees were uprooted and washed swiftly along in the swirling water, as it rushed over rocks in the mountain streams. In recent years an old half rotted buggy was found in the woods far from any road and partly buried in sand which indicated that it had been washed there, and it was attributed to the 1916 flood.

The lower floor of the "White Water Inn' at Jocassee, on the Oconee County side, was submerged and the visitors had to flee to the mountain behind the house for safety. By two o'clock Monday morning a large steel bridge over Keowee River near Chapman's Ford had washed away. The farms along both sides of the river suffered a great loss of crops. Some of the bridges on Keowee and Seneca Rivers remained intact on account of the spread of the water into other streams.

In 1917 a Highway Commission was created for Pickens County, consisting of three members appointed by the Governor upon recommendation of the County Delegation. The Commissioners filed a joint bond of $25,000 approved by the Clerk of Court. In 1918 the successor of any Commissioner was required to file a bond of $10,000. Premiums on these bonds were paid from the tax levy terms of the Commissioners until their duties were completed. Each Commissioner was paid $3 per day for his service, not exceeding $300 per year. Vacancies were filled by the Governor upon recommendation of the Delegation. The Commission organized by electing one of its member chairman, who also acted as treasurer. The treasurer's additional bond was $10,000, to be approved by the Clerk of Court. The Commissioners also elected and set the salary of a clerk, who was not required to be a member of the Commission. The clerk gave bond for $5000, which must be approved by the Commission. The Commissioners were also empowered to employ and set the salary of an engineer and such assistants as was necessary.

It was the duty of the Commission after advertising for 30 days to offer for sale the $250,000 in bonds which had been issued by the County for permanent road improvement. The bonds were to be sold in blocks of not less than $5000, or at the discretion of the Commission. Before any of the money could be expended the Commission was required to have the engineer survey and locate the roads for permanent improvement, and any road laid out by the Commission was deemed a public road. The County Supervisor was to cooperate by supplying machinery and convict labor. There was a great need for better roads.

The Main roads in Pickens County were top-soiled before the day of surface treating, and paving began. And many improvements were made in bridges all over the county under the supervision of James B. Craig, Supervisor 1910-1919.

In the decade between 1910-1920 all of the shade trees

were removed from the streets and sidewalks of Pickens and the sidewalks in front of the stores were paved. A local electric company, which was run by water power, was installed at the Clement's grist mill a few miles west of town and supplied the town with electricity when the weather, and water conditions were favorable. It was called "The Ivy Light and Water Company." It was owned by Mr. A. M. Morris and Company.

Telephones were becoming general over the country and many homes had radioes that they ran with a Ford battery. They would use the battery in the car all day, and at home in the radio at night. K.D.K.A. at Pittsburg was about the only station they could get, but they worked it overtime.

Victrolas and phonographs had long been the prized possession of many families who had no other musical instrument. The first of those had been used with ear phones, later with an amplifier horn attached. Conditions were right generally the same all over the country. The young people went buggy riding with their dates without opposition by that time, and lawn parties in summer, and socials and dances in the winter were in order for pastime. While these were not obviously chaperoned they were usually held in a good home where parents felt that their young people were reasonably safe.

Baseball, basketball, and football were becoming increasingly popular and all of the high schools tried to encourage them by employing teacher-coaches. Junior-senior receptions in high schools had their beginning in Pickens County back in that time. And many romances developed from one town to another.

In 1914-1915 a state of war was brewing in Europe that affected American trade. The price of cotton dropped from fifteen cents a pound to six cents.

Pickens County adopted the plan of individuals buying from one to ten bales of cotton to boost the price. Almost every yard had a bale of cotton in it. A tense feeling prevailed. There was talk of war.

On April 3, 1917 tall head lines appeared in all the newspapers declaring a "State of War." President Woodrow Wilson asked for an Army of 500,0000 men upon the Universal Service Plan. The President's address follows; in part:

"I have called the Congress into extraordinary session because there are serious, very serious choices of policy to be made, and made immediately, which it was neither right nor constitutionally permissable that I should assume the responsibility of making.

"On the third of February last I laid before you the extraordinary announcement of the Imperial German Government that on and after the first day of February it was its purpose to put aside all restraints of law or humanity and use its submarines to sink every vessel that sought to approach either the ports of Great Britain and Ireland, or the western coasts of Europe, or any of the ports controlled by enemies of Germany within the Mediterranean." His speech continued at length. .... "The German Government denies the right of neutrals to use arms within the areas of the sea which it has prescribed, even in the defense of their own rights. Armed neutrality is ineffectual at best, but under existing circumstances we are almost certain to be forced into war.

"With a profound sense of the solemn and even tragical step I am taking, but in unhesitating constitutional duty I advise the Congress to declare the recent course of the imperial German Government to be nothing less than a state of war against the United States Government. ...."

The first American Armed ship that sailed had been sunk by a submarine in March and several of the crew had perished. And before that, for a year or two America was becoming involved.

160

After President Wilson's address to Congress on that memorable day of April 3rd, 1917 he left the Capitol and the congressmen and senators reconvened and made the following joint resolution:

"That the President be, and is hereby authorized and directed to take immediate steps not only to put the country in a thorough state of defense, but also to exert all of its power and employ all of its resources to carry on war against the imperial German government and to bring the conflict to a successful termination."

Plans for the mobilization of a war-time Army and Navy got underway immediately. Huge cantonments were erected at convenient places all over the United States for training soldiers, and conscription began in earnest. Camp Jackson, Columbia; Camp Sevier, at Greenville; and Camp Wadsworth at Spartanburg were the ones nearest Pickens County.

By the early part of 1918 many of our boys were in Europe. Liberty Bonds were being sold on the streets and in the stores. "Make the world safe for Democracy" was the slogan. A new group of songs was composed overnight and everybody was singing them: "Over There, Keep the Home Fires Burning, I Didn't Raise My Boy To Be a Soldier, There's a Long Trail a Winding," and many others. There were dark days when news came from the front that some of our men had been wounded or killed. There were days when the church congregations in Pickens County met for mid-week, mid-morning prayer services that all would end well.

And finally the Armistice was signed November 11, 1918. It would be impossible to give full credit to all of the men who were wounded or lost in the conflict. But there are two Pickens County men still living among us in 1958 that deserve to be honored.

Mr. Jesse D. Gillespie, Treasurer of Pickens County since

161

1925 is one of these. Mr. Gillespie was a Corporal in Company K. Twenty-eighth Infantry, First Division. The death certificate in his possession states that "he died with honor in the service of his country" on May 28, 1918. He also has a telegram to his relatives from the War Department in June of that year stating that his name appeared in the official casualty list.

The Cantigny Drive was on during the last day of May 1918 and Corporal Gillespie was sent out with a detail of five men on outpost duty. They established themselves in adjoining shell holes that offered small protection and began filling bags with dirt to shield them further from the enemy fire. Two of Mr. Gillespie's comrades were soon killed outright, and a third badly wounded started crawling back to the American lines.

Suddenly, a high explosive stuck the outpost throwing metal fragments in all directions. Corporal Gillespie's right leg was shattered above the knee, his other leg was wounded and one arm and hand badly mangled. He remembered some extra shoe strings in his pocket and with the help of the remaining unwounded comrade he bound up his arm and hand and fixed a tourniquet on his bad leg. In a few minutes his helper was killed and he and the other wounded soldier were the only Americans that remained. They tried to drag themselves toward the American lines and Corporal Gillespie was forced to amputate the balance of his shattered leg with his pocket knife before he could drag himself. After five days of unbearable thirst and suffering he was picked up. He stayed in French and American hospitals overseas for eleven months before he was brought back on a stretcher to Fort McPherson, Georgia for eighteen more months of hospital treatment. Twenty-nine months in all.

He left Fort McPherson on crutches and spent the next thirteen months studying for office work, as he knew he would never be physically able for any other kind. He was elected as Pickens County Treasurer in 1925, the office he still holds. Mr. Gillespie is married and has three sons.

The other Pickens County man is Clarence R. Porter, known to his friends as "Slim" Porter. He has served as a barber in both Easley and Pickens.

In the book published by the United States War Department listing soldiers who have been awarded Distinguished Services Crosses "for extraordinary heroism in action" and stating reasons for awards, appears the following:

"Clarence R. Porter, Pickens, S. C. Private, Company D. 119th Infantry, 30th Division. While his company was making an attack on the Hindenburg Line, he continued a covering fire with his Lewis gun. In spite of two wounds from which he was suffering he remained at his post until his company succeeded in reaching the line."

The Distinguished Service Cross is the second highest decoration that may be awarded a soldier of the U. S. Army, and comparatively few have won it. Mr. Porter was the only soldier from Pickens County and the only one in his company who was awarded this medal in War I. He was also awarded the British Military Medal and recommended for French and Belgium decorations. General Haig, Commander of the British Army pinned his country's medal on Private Porter in France.

While Pvt. Porter's wounds were being dressed, he noticed a distinctive birth-mark on the physician's hand. He did not know the doctor, only that he was an American. A few years, after the war, when Mr. Porter was running a Barber Shop in Easley, S. C. Dr. C. M. Tripp, an Easley physician, came in for service and Mr. Porter noticed the same birthmark on his hand. They became better acquainted immediately and reminisced over their experiences on the battlefield in France. Mr. Porter married Miss Gertrude Finley and has three children.

There was a strong bond of loyalty between the boys who came back from France. Many of their friends had died on the battlefield, many had died in the violent flu epidemic that struck in the Fall of 1918, many were forced to spend the rest of their lives as cripples, or detained for months, or years, in some Veterans' Hospital. When the American Legion was organized most of them joined. An American Legion meeting place was established in every town. A substantial brick "hut" was built in Pickens (now the home of the Pickens Sentinel), in after years when it was sold to the Sentinel another American Legion house was built. The mothers, wives, and daughters formed an American Legion Auxiliary, and it was the same in other towns in Pickens County.

In 1921 two Pickens County companies were organized as units of the 118th Infantry Regiment with headquarters at Easley. later, through a W.P.A. project their Armory was built.

In 1914 Pickens County had appropriated $150 for the promotion of Club Work in rural communities, to be distributed by the Superintendent of Education. In 1916 an appropriation of $600 was made for Home Demonstration Work. The number of County Agents in the State varied from year to year as long as the provision of supplementary funds was left to the counties. Since 1929 the State has appropriated a sufficient amount to insure each county one Farm and one Home Agent.

Miss Sarah Cureton has done outstanding work in supervising Home Demonstration work in Pickens County.

In 1926 Mrs. A. P. Raines, Route 1 Easley sold $1436.-90 plants and vegetables from her garden. Some were shipped to other states from advertising her plants in the Farm Bulletin. Other women too numerous to call by name have attended Club meetings faithfully and added much to the beauty of their homes and communities, in every section of the county.

In 1920 Mr. T. A. Bowen, Pickens County Agent, organized the first "Boys' Community Club" in South Carolina at Long Branch in Pickens County. The 4H Club was a new organization then to promote and encourage better farm and home economics among the youth of the Nation.

Rocky Bottom 4H Club Camp in Pickens County, South Carolina was the first 4H Camp in the United States. It was established in 1925.

The Rocky Bottom Club Camp is located seventeen miles north of Pickens on the Pickens-Brevard Highway, which was built just before the camp opened. The late Wade H. Chastain gave twenty-three acres of land, in his generous public spirited way, and others were inspired to do their part. The camp was first constructed for approximately $7000. Of this money $1000 was appropriated by the Pickens County legislative delegation, $1000 by the Picknes County Board of Education, and $1000 by Bernard M. Baruch of New York. The other $4000 was raised by the citizens of Pickens County.

The place that had been a mountain jungle in 1925 soon turned into a wide clearing with a Club House kitchen, Assembly and Dining Halls, a girls' dormitory to house 175, and a boys' barracks with space for 300. At first a stream was dammed up to make a natural swimming pool, later a larger concrete pool was built. Nine rattlesnakes were killed on the grounds that first summer while the camp was being built. After the crowds started coming snakes were not often seen around the place.

The first trustees of the camp were T. R. O'Dell, chairman; T. A. Bowen, Wade H. Chastain, George H. Hendricks, Ben Frank Freeman, and Charles L. Cureton. When Mr. Chastain died his son, Furman Chastain, succeeded him.

165

Wm. Ponder, Jr., succeeded Mr. George Hendricks, and L. H. Ballentine succeeded Mr. Cureton.

Mr. T. A. Bowen built a private cottage near the dormitories for the use of supervisors, officers, and friends of the camp. As time passed lots were sold on the adjoining property and many cottages were built for vacation homes.

In the summer of 1926, after the 4H encampment was held early in June, a Boys' School and Camp was held at the 4H Club from June 21, to August 1st. Mr. F. Van Clayton, a former Superintendent of Education and at that time Superintendent of the Pickens High School was the head Counciler. Other instructors at the camp were: Mr. L. L. Wright, Superintendent of the Honea Path School, Principal Godfrey of the Abbeville School, and Mr. C. A. Robinson, Athletic Coach of the Pickens High School. Mrs. W. C. Newton of Pickens was the Camp Mother and Dietitian. The Camp had Sunday School and preaching every Sunday, literary classes five days a week, and athletic and supervised hikes six days a week. The student body was limited to one hundred.

In 1940 Pickens County appropriated $3800 for a Farm and Home Demonstration, Agricultural Building, and $150 for 4H Club boys and girls. The building was erected on the Court House Square in Pickens and named "The Bowen Building" in honor of Mr. T. A. Bowen who had done so much in farm, home, and 4H Club work in Pickens County.

Many organizations from all parts of South Carolina have used and enjoyed the Rocky Bottom Camp. Bankers, Press Association, and many religious groups have held their conventions there when the 4H Clubs were not using it.

In 1940 Mr. Bowen suggested having a "Goodwill Supper" there in the late Summer or early Fall of each year for men of Pickens County and prominent visitors from all over South Carolina, and other states who were promoting the best interests of the State and Nation. Many Governors and others in leading positions have been entertained there. Mr. Bowen retired as active manager in 1950 and Mr. J. R. Wood, County Agent, succeeded him.

Another camp in the Pickens County mountains that did a good work the several years that it lasted was Camp John B. Adger, owned and operated by the State Y.M.C.A. It bore the name of a Belton, S. C. man who because of his interest in the boys of South Carolina purchased the land about 1920 and gave it to the State Committee to establish such a camp. The propery consisted of 163½ acres of land thickly wooded with enough cleared space for buildings, athletic fields, and gardens. It was an old house place and there were many apple trees surroundings the original log cabin. It was located in the heart of the Blue Ridge Mountains about two miles above the old Price Grist Mill and the pool Pickens County young people once knew as "Gauly." A one way road led up from Gauly to the camp, a good two miles if you walked it, and up hill every step of the way. Tradition said it had once been the road from Pickens District to Asheville, N. C., with a toll gate near the old Price mill. The "Hog Drovers' road, it was called.

The equipment of Camp Adger consisted of one large cabin used for headquarters, library, and dining hall; six small cabins for boys, a swimming pool, orchard, garden, barn and big play ground. Each cabin had iron cots and mats. The meals were served family style in the big dining room. Forty or fifty boys could stay at one time and the expense was only nine dollars a week. A happy combination of work and play was arranged. Boys did not have to be members of the Y.M.C.A. to come and different age groups were scheduled to come at different times.

The Rev. T. B. Lanham, for many years State Secretary of the Y.M.C.A. helped to direct the Camp, and acted as its Headmaster several seasons. His influence will long be remembered.

Under the Smith-Hughes Law for Vocational Training in Agriculture, three four-weeks schools were conducted during the summer of 1926 in South Carolina. One of these was at Six Mile in Pickens County. Ninety boys from fourteen years up were enrolled. They were housed in the Baptist Academy buildings and paid $15 each for the full four weeks. There were no other fees.

Classes began at 8:00 A.M. and were over for the day at 12:30. The afternoons were given to inspecting nearby farms, orchards, and poultry yards, with some time for athletics.

The Smith-Hughes Schools were an attempt to reach boys who had few privileges, and give them the opportunity to study the essentials of good agriculture.

SIX MILE

Dr. and Mrs. David E. Peek came to Six Mile in 1918. They had only been married a few months, but they were destined to wield a big influence over the Six Mile Community, and Pickens County at large. They were natives of Western, North Carolina. Mrs. Peek was a graduate of Cullowee and her home was on the banks of the Tuckaseigee River. She was Miss Florence Wike, the daughter of Mr. and Mrs. W. D. Wike.

Dr. Peek was born at Erastus, N. C., the son of Mr. and Mrs. Buford Peek. He received his early education at Sylva, N. C. Later, he attended Carson-Newman College, at Jefferson City, Tenn., for two years, and then went to Medical College at Emory University, Atlanta. After his internship in Atlanta, and Army duty among the soldiers in Atlanta hospitals during the great flu epidemic he came directly to Six Mile. He spent a few years practicing medicine over the Six Mile country, and then in 1925 he established the first hospital in Pickens County.

Some people live a great life in a short span of years, a life that continues in the minds and hearts of those who knew them best; such a man was the late Dr. David E. Peek of Six Mile.

Perhaps no one knows when the dream of a hospital in a rural community first came to him. It could be that some patient, who died for the need of surgery, gave him the inspiration, or some patient in a lonely isolated cabin where there were no facilities for taking care of the sick. As he rode the long miles home on some bitter winter night perhaps he thought that there in the shadow of Six Mile Mountain was a broad field for an institution serving humanity.

Early at night on March 13, 1929, after a rainy day, a cyclone struck Six Mile. Several houses were completely destroyed and nine lives were immediately wiped out, and a dozen others suffered various injuries. One moment Six Mile was a little town of peaceful homes, and the next it was a place of horror with survivors hurrying out in the rain with lanterns, as soon as the noise of wind and flying timbers had subsided, to look for their friends and loved ones. Their power line which came from Cateechee had been destroyed.

Two Garrett families were almost completely wiped out. The dead were: Deputy Sheriff, Nelse Garrett, his wife, and three children.

In another home close by Mrs. Tillman Garrett and three daughters were killed. The dead were tenderly brought in out of the rain and the injured were taken into the hospital for treatment. The hospital at that time was in a residence type building, next door to Dr. Peek's home. Every home was opened for the sufferers.

It continued to rain the next day, and although the roads were unpaved and mud was ankle deep, hundreds of people came from a distance to offer their assistance, and to help search the debris for other possible victims.

This was the greatest tragedy that Pickens County has ever had, and it was a sad day when the nine caskets bearing the remains of the storm victims were buried in two big graves in the Six Mile churchyard.

The Baptist Academy at Six Mile had closed and Dr. Peek bought the girls' dorimitory and remodeled it into a forty bed hospital. He had fourteen doctors on the staff, all of the Pickens County doctors, and some from Greenville, to insure the patients the best service. All of the equipment was strictly modern. The institution was incorporated as "Dr. Peek's Hospital" and the following trustees were elected: Mrs. Gertrude Mathews, Easley; C. C. Boroughs, Norris; J. D. Vickery, Central; J. A. Roper, Six Mile; E. F. Cantrell, Liberty; Mrs. Myrta Stevenson, and Frank McFall, Pickens.

Outside of the $700 per year rent that the trustees paid Dr. Peek all other income from the hospital went for its improvement and upkeep. A grant for charity patients came from a county appropriation. Besides Dr. Peek's practice he farmed and raised cattle. Each summer he left another doctor in charge of his hospital for a few weeks and went to New York or one of the other big medical centers to study the newest discoveries in medicine.

In 1930 when Dr. Peek's forty bed hospital was completed several girls in the Six Mile community asked for nurse's training. A few were taken in under the tutelage of Mrs. Nell Gaines Dillard who had been the head nurse since 1927. Mrs. Dillard came to Six Mile as Miss Nell Gaines and remained as Mrs. J. Austin Dillard, after she married a Six Mile man.

Two nurses graduated in 1933, Miss Willie Grace Mullinax, and Miss Jessie Mae Sullivan. Appropriate graduating exercises were held at the First Baptist Church in Pickens, S. C.

Five graduated in 1934, Miss Lucile Stewart, Miss Elizabeth Jones, Miss Ruby White, Miss Mildred Miller, and Miss Mattie Jo McWhorter.

In 1935 there were three, Miss Ruth Mauldin, Miss Vella Duvall, and Miss Julia Townes. The classes were discontinued after that.

There was always a gracious atmosphere around Dr. Peek's hospital and home and he and Mrs. Peek enjoyed entertaining the Medical Society and their many friends.

Another dream was growing in Dr. Peek's mind, to put a hospital on top of Six Mile Mountain. It was only three miles from Six Mile and the elevation was 1650 feet while the village was only 825 feet. A road was built up the mountain and a large rustic house where they entertained friends on several occasions, but the hospital was never built. Such a project takes time, and time was not for him.

Dr. Peek was stricken while going about his duties and died March 17, 1942. He left his wife and three children. He was a great humanitarian and a prominent physician. He belonged to many State and National Medical Societies, and was a member of the Alpha Kappa Kappa Fraternity.

The heirs of the late Dr. Peek sold their hospital to the Baptist Hospital Board of Columbia. The building was purchased by subscription of interested citizens in Pickens County and donated to the Baptists to help keep the hospital open. It immediately became "The Six Mile Hospital." It was accepted for the Baptist Hospital by Dr. W. M. Whitesides, Supt. of the Baptist Hospital in Columbia. And as such it continued to function.

Chapter 15

Some of the industries built in Pickens County between 1915-1930 were: Easley, 1923 Alice Manufacturing Company, with Mr. E. H. Shanklin, president.

Easley 1924, Carolina Times Publishing Company.

Easley 1925, Taylor - Colquitt Company, poles and cross-ties.

Pickens 1924: Pickens Hardwood Manufacturing Company.

Pickens 1927: Appalachian Lumber Company, at the present site of the Poinsett Manufacturing Company.

Pickens 1926: Nalley Lumber Company.

Pickens 1929: Blue Ridge Milling Company.

Six Mile: Six Mile Gin Company.

Between 1915-1930 Pickens County boasted a modern trans-mountain highway at a cost of $300,000, the road paid for out of taxes as it was built. A good road twenty-six miles from east to west across the county, hard surfacing of many roads about to begin.

Apples and peaches were grown successfully in several commercial orchards, privately owned.

Pickens County rated second in the State in poultry shipments.

Some farmers boasted a yield of more than one hundred bushels of corn per acre, and a bale of cotton per acre.

Pickens County boys and girls were winning top places in spelling, oratory, and all kinds of athletics, and through the efforts of Miss Will Lou Gray of Columbia adult education had begun.

After World War 1 there was a great deal of talk about getting back to normalcy but the "War that was to end all Wars" had accomplished little. There had been a great loss of life and the expense of the War ran around forty-two billion dollars. People began to think and talk about larger sums of money than ever before. There was Nation-wide speculation.

Woodrow Wilson died. Harding came into office and committed many ungentlemanly deeds before his death, then Coolidge and Hoover were elected before the great financial crisis of 1929. Some called it the "Hoover Depression."

1932 was characterized by great economic uncertainty. First class letter postage went to three cents. It had been two cents since 1884. (It changed to four cents August first 1958). Ford V8 came on the market, price $460. The Democrats endorsed Franklin D. Roosevelt for President of the United States.

By March 1933 when Roosevelt was inaugurated fifteen million people in the United States were out of work. Some were in desperate circumstances, and some were lazy and willing to take an unfair advantage of the charity that became almost a by-word, even in Pickens County.

Roosevelt's campaign had been for a "new deal" and when he was elected substantial Democratic majorities went to Congress and the United States Senate with him. They set up many organizations and most of them were called by initials. Perhaps the W.P.A. (Works Progress Administration) helped Pickens County more than some of the others. It gave many people work and added new buildings and bridges that we might not have had so soon.

The Bank Holiday was the greatest blow Pickens County had. Ten banks closed and only the old "Pickens Bank" opened in good standing.

When the FERA (Federal Relief Administration) was superseded by the WPA, its unexpended funds were entrusted to the Governors of the states for relief of the unemployed. In South Carolina a temporary department of Public Welfare was set up to administer this relief. Pickens County participated until funds were exhausted in 1937. Then the permanent State Department of Public Welfare was created. Pickens County's Department of Public Welfare is housed in a building on Ann Street in Pickens, with Mrs. Nona Lee Jennings, Director, and several assistants (1958).

After the new bank was built on the corner of Main and Pendleton Stretes in Pickens, and became the South Carolina National Bank it had a room in the back that was used for a year or two as the Postoffice. Then when Frank McFall built the present (1958) Postoffice building, the back room of the bank became a barber shop until the bank needed the extra space.

One day in the 1930's the South Carolina National Bank had a visit from bank robbers. It was a regulation hold-up in every respect. The bandit appeared as a potential customer at the noon hour when some of the workers were out to lunch. Then his accomplice strolled in and before the two bankers and a secretary knew what was happening they were covered by fire-arms and demanded to lie on the floor until the bandits hurriedly helped themselves to a sizeable amount of cash and got away. They were never caught and the money was never recovered, except by insurance.

The Appalachian Lumber Company that came to Pickens in 1927 did not last long. They built a narrow gauge extension of the Pickens Railroad back into Eastatoe to haul lumber, but they failed during the depression, and the railroad was discontinued. No sign of it remains.

They were followed by another lumber company that also failed to function. In 1939 they sold their holdings to the Singer Sewing Machine Company which established a

subsidiary at Pickens and called it "The Poinsett Lumber &
Manufacturing Company." They employed about 750 workers in plant and office and added much to the industrial life
of Pickens County.

Mr. and Mrs. T. J. Mitchell of Michigan came to
Pickens in 1939 when Mr. Mitchell became Manager of
the Poinsett Plant. When Mr. Mitchell retired in 1956 Mr.
W. L. Irwin became Plant Manager and he and Mrs. Irwin
moved to Pickens.

Along in the 1930's there was a great deal of talk and
advertising about the iodine content in South Carolina vegetables. South Carolina automobile tags were stamped "The
Iodine State." This did not last long because it caused too
many embarrassing questions when South Carolinians were
on motor trips.

About that time a negro man named Will Ferguson
had a grocery store in Pickens on the corner formerly occupied by the Harvey Richey store, later by a T. L. Bivens
store, and in 1958 by the Ansel Nealy store.

It was a gathering place for taxi drivers and Paris Size-
more, Lem Rosamond, Big Boy Sloan and others could be
found there.

Ferguson kept a good line of country produce and advertised in a unique way. One summer he got out a fan that
bore a tempting list: "country ham, fryers, green beans, fresh
corn, tomatoes, peaches, and cantaloupes."

And down below the list this little couplet was printed:

"They make you strong. They'll make you fat. They'll
eat right where you hold 'em at."

175

LAKE ISAQUEENA

One of the principal features of the 23,000 acre Clemson College Land Use Project was started in 1934 by the U.S. Department of Agriculture to develop tracts of worn out land to the economic and social welfare of the people of Pickens County.

Lake Isaqueena was completed in 1938 by damming several streams to provide fishing, boating, and picnic facilities to the people living within a thirty mile radius of Clemson College.

A beach was provided, bath houses were built, and a diving stand was erected by the time the lake was completed.

At first it was a beautiful lake and the water was clear. Then with the first heavy rains a patch of turgid, muddy water was observed at the head of the lake. As more rains came and the inflows increased they advanced into the center of the lake, until all of the water had a strange murky color.

After the exceptionally heavy rains of the late summer of 1940 the lake was pronounced undesirable as a swimming and boating resort. It had become a mass of muddy water.

CCC Camps were part of the Roosevelt program. The first one in Pickens County was located at Liberty. The boys were trained in conservation work. The Camp was moved to the Table Rock area, and under the supervision of Mr. Norman House Table Rock State Park was developed.

The Park is located at the foot of the mountains in Pickens County fifteen miles north of the town of Pickens. It is one of the recreational parks of the Southern system. It contains more than 2000 acres of land and has Table Rock Mountain as a back-drop.

An Indian legend of a great Chief who in time immemorial sat on the stool (a small adjoining mountain) and ate from the great Table Rock enhances the glamour of the scene. And the trails and by-paths that lead to the top of the mountain are a never ending source of interest for botanists and nature lovers who are always finding new plants and ferns.

A number of grills and picnic areas have been placed along the forest paths, and a fish hatchery is also a point of interest.

A mountain stream was dammed to make a big lake for swimming and boating, and there is a diving stand and a lifeguard always on call.

There are more than a dozen cabins for vacationing familities, and Sunday School teachers from the towns hold Sunday classes for the campers.

There is a picturesque lodge where meals are served, with a spacious room and a hi-fie for games and dances.

The park superintendent's home is near the lodge. M. T. Roper, R. A. Cole, Ernest Cooler, and Mr. Jones have served as Park Superintendents.

RURAL ELECTRIFICATION

Rural electrification was set up by an Act of the General Assembly in South Carolina in 1935. The Blue Ridge Electric Co-op Inc., was organized in Pickens County on the 8th of October 1940. Service to farmers has resulted in expansion in many lines of farm and home work.

In May 1953, Mr. T. Ross O'Dell, at that time president of the Blue Ridge Co-op, obtained the loan for a modern office building in Pickens at a cost of $165,000. A branch office was located at Westminster in Oconee County.

With the coming of good roads a greater need arose for forest fire protection and fire towers were built at various points in the county. One is on Sassafras Mountain, one is on Glassy Mountain, and another on Woodall Mountain.

Many unusual discoveries have been made as the county developed. Along in the 1940's while digging a well Mr. E. N. McJunkin of the Ambler section ran into well preserved timbers twenty-two feet beneath the surface of the ground. The soil was solid red clay. One oak log was eighteen feet long with the bark still on it and completely sound.

Mr. McJunkin bought his farm more than fifty years ago, $2.50 per acre. He cleared the land himself and there was no sign of a house place on it. It looked like the remains of a mine shaft, but there is no record of mining in that section and Mr. McJunkin's ancestors had lived near by for a long time.

When T-Model Fords were popular and lots of fellows were getting a broken arm from cranking them, a local wit in Pickens County wrote a letter to "Henry Ford" on a bet, and got an answer. The letter and the answer were as follows:

Mr. Henry Ford, Detroit, Michigan, Dear Sir: "It gives me great pleasure to have the honor and the occasion to write to you, you being the founder and the manufacturer of the world famous Tin-Lizzie—Flivver—Jitney, and so on. Famous for rough riding, backfiring, and high kicking. I am not finding fault with them, understand; for I have driven one five or six years. The only trouble was I got hold of one that wasn't thoroughly broke.

I had kept it so long that I had all the confidence in the world in it but it turned on me like a Judas's kiss. The other day I started it and it kind of backfired, but me being an old Ford driver I walked around and cut the spark off and went back to crank it, only to have my arm dislocated and broke at the same time.

I got cold feet and ran and left the thing backfirin', and it may be still doing it for all I know. I thought I would write you so you could be on the lookout for it, as I guess it has gone back to the herd.

It's a good thing that Fords are not like milk cows or you might have trouble selling the ones that kick. But after all I can't find much fault with them as fifteen cents worth of gas, a dime's worth of oil, and a good head of water will run one all day. Now if this Ford comes home please take the kick out and return it. Randolph Rose took the kick out of licker, you ought to be able to take it out of a Ford. Yours respectfully, C.H.

The reply came back promptly—

"Dear Sir: I have your letter telling me about one of my automobiles kicking you. It seems strange that you should complain of a Ford with a kick in it when everybody is complaining they can't seem to find anything with a kick in it. Neither can I understand why you complain about a little thing like your arm being broke when the whole blame country is broke.

However, I'm glad you wrote me for I want us to be good friends and I'm going to take you into my confidence. The Ford you got is undoubtedly not one of our best. Unless what happened to you was something like a similar incident. A man we will call John wrote to me wanting $300 damages because he said one of our Fords had kicked him, broke his arm and skinned his head. Upon investigation at his hospital we learned that his wife followed him to the door that morning wanting him to cut some stove wood and when he replied that he wasn't taking the axe to work with him she settled with him, then and there.

I'm not accusing you because you may be a single man, but you mentioned knowing Randolph Rose. He used to wind up his advertisements, 'I thank you'. And what he should have said was 'I tank you'. Or would that fit your case?

Since you mentioned milk cows, are you sure that it wasn't a cow that kicked you?"

Yours respectfully—Henry Ford.

179

WORLD WAR II

Another War started in Europe in the late 1930's, and when Pearl Harbor was bombed December 7, 1940 we became a part of the second World War. Again there was rationing of commodities, and all of the attendant inconveniences of War, and the deep sadness of seeing our boys begin the long trek overseas again. This time there was a difference in the patriotism that had been so exuberant before. Perhaps it was tinged with skepticism. When would it all end? But the boys went bravely on and many of them gave their lives in the conflict. About one hundred men from Pickens County lost their lives, in World War II and two of them won Congressional Medals of Honor.

Private Furman L. Smith, of Central, was the first South Carolinian to receive the Congressional Medal of Honor in World War II. The Nation's highest military honor was awarded Private Smith, posthumously for stubbornly holding his post when the enemy overran his position.

Lt. Col. Filmore K. Mears was among the witnesses and had seen two of his sargents fall with wounds. They were lying in the path of the advancing enemy. "Smith stood between them," Col. Mears reported. "Then with the barrage bursting around him I saw him drag the non-coms to a shell hole.." He knew that his deed had drawn the enemy fire.

"I saw him crawl with only his M-1 to another shell hole and continue to fire clip for clip." He was killed in part of the heaviest fighting to take place in Italy, on a slope near Lanuinoo. May 31, 1944.

The award of the Medal of Honor was made to Mr. and Mrs. Charles Leonard Smith by Major General John H. Hester of Camp Croft, on Jan. 17, 1945.

Since that time an American Cemetery in Italy has been named in honor of Private Furman L. Smith, who received a Congressional Medal of Honor in World War II. Post 141 of the Six Mile American Legion was named in his honor, and also a highway.

The following members of the American Legion acted as pallbearers when his body was brought home for burial in the Pleasant Hill Cemetery 1948: Melvin Stephens, Roy Merck, James Kelly, Charles Alexander, Earl Loftis, Lloyd Hendricks, Noah Evatt, and Leonard Merck.

Another Pickens County soldier who won a Congressional Medal of Honor, posthumously in World War 11, was Pfc William H. McWhorter, Liberty, S. C.

McWhorter died in action in the Phillipines December 3, 1944, while defending his country beyond the call of duty.

It was on the Island of Yevte during the Phillipine invasion. Pfc McWhorter and Pfc Brooks of Alabama were operating a machine gun. It was jungle country and the Japanese were trying to rout them out of their position.

Pfc. Brooks said: "Just as we halted them I saw something fly through the air and realized it was a brick of TNT with a lighted fuse. McWhorter caught it and turned aside before it exploded and killed him."

The Congressional Medal of Honor was delivered to the wife, Mrs. Bethel McWhorter, at the home of his parents Mr. and Mrs. John O. McWhorter, Liberty, S. C. October 3, 1945.

Pfc McWhorter's body was brought home and buried with military honors at Westview Cemetery, Liberty, S. C., February 5, 1949. The following friends served as pallbearers: Joe Gantt, Eugene Garrison, Carl Allgood, Marvin McKinney, Robert Traber, and Marvin Smith, and the American Legion acted as honorary escort.

EASLEY HIGH SCHOOL

A $240,000 modern high school was built in Easley in the 1940's. A new Postoffice was built on the corner where the former high school had stood. Easley had a Northside school, a Westend school, and later built an Eastside school.

Easley was a growing town with many stores and automobile agencies. New banks were opened. A new City Hall was built, the Pickens County Library, a new Easley Hotel, a large new moving picture theater, which the Armistead family owned and operated. The Home Building and Loan Association had changed to the Easley Building and Loan Association. A new water and light plant was establisehd. Other industries were: Food Products; Quick Freeze Locker Service; McCravy and Freeman, Fertilizers; Easley Fertilizer; Easley Ice and Fuel Company; Farmers' Warehouse; Easley Roller Mill; gins, and lumber yards.

Textile products besides cotton mills, Artex, Inc., Hudson Narow Fabric Mills, tapes and webbing; Pinnacle Mills, yarn; Chenille and Bedspread companies.

The Easley Progress had become a widely read newspaper, with Mr. Julien D. Wyatt, Mrs. Ora Kirkley, and later Mr. Rogers as editors.

Many new homes and churches grew up along with the town to meet the needs of the growing population.

SIX MILE CHURCH

On January 31, 1943 a new brick church, complete for worship services, was dedicated at Six Mile. This is a Baptist church. For years the membership, which extends over a large surrounding community, had realized their need for a larger and better church building. The church at Six Mile was one hundred years old 1936.

Under the leadership of their very able pastor, the Rev. F. S. Childress, plans began to take shape in 1928. A building fund was started with Dr. D. E. Peek as treasurer. Other friends and churches in various communties helped Each member was asked to give at least one dollar, and the ladies devised many fund raising projects.

By 1931 the cash, notes, and pledges amounted to more than $3000 and the Official Board and church members voted to start a new building As the building grew they continued to raise funds to apply on special objects.

The membership pulled together in every detail, even to the actual building of the church. Mr. W. F. Turner was employed to supervise the workers, and with the exception of the bricklayers all work was free. Land owners in the surrounding community cut trees and hauled them to saw mills to provide lumber. It would be impossible to give credit to all the names of those who helped in this splendid cause. The women of the church, individually, and through their organizations worked equally as hard as the men

Six Mile has given missionaries to the foreign fields. At present John A. Roper, Jr. is among them.

In 1958 the church is adding a $30,000 educational building.

OLD BAPTIST CHURCHES

The Twelve Mile River Baptist Association was organized October 3, 1829 at Secona Church in Pickens District, near the present town of Pickens. These churches came together from the Saluda Baptist Association; Secona, 1789, Liberty 1780-90, Keowee 1791, Oolenoy 1789, Crossroads 1795, Peter's Creek 1798, Antioch, 1798. (Dates stand for about the time they were organized).

The Twelve Mile Association listed churches at their

annual meetings in the following years from what is now Oconee County, some from Greenville, and Anderson Counties, and a few from North Carolina.

The following churches with their dates of joining the Association are only those in the present area of Pickens County. Perhaps some of them had meetnig houses for a while before they joined the Association, but they were more likely to be supplied with a pastor if they joined. These dates are copied directly from the minutes of The Twelve Mile River Baptist Association:

"1836, Six Mile, 24 members, Bryan Boroughs probably first pastor.

1837, Mount Carmel, Dacusville, 15 members, John Kennemore.

1846, Holly Springs (first called Bethlehem), 34 mem., M. Chastain.

1848, Pleasant Hill, 29 mem., Lewis Finley.

1850, Mountain Grove, 19 Mem., M. Chastain.

1850, Enon, 19 Mem., W. B. Singleton.

"1857, Griffin, 20 Mem. W. B. Singleton." (Note: It is believed by some that there was a meeting house at this place for a long time, organized by the Baptist Missionary preacher Elnathan Davis. He died in 1821 and is buried there. However, there is no record of what his church was called. And Griffin, as "Griffin Church" was named in 1856 when Sargent Griffin gave the land and requested that the church be named for him.

A small frame church was built with two glass windows, and the others wooden shutters. The first baptising was Aug. 26, 1857 in Sargent Griffin's Mill pond. A better church was built 1880, and still another in 1909, which burned 1948. The present beautiful church and pastorium were built in 1949. And the women of the church did a remarkable job in helping to raise the money for this project of love. Their efforts were similar to Six Mile.

Returning to the records of the Twelve Mile Association:

"1859, George's Creek, 13 Mem., L. Von. A year later they had 40 mem.

1862, Saluda Hill, 67 Mem., J. W. Blythe.

1865 Shady Grove, 28 Mem., C. Roper.

1868 Walnut Grove, 12 Mem. J. H. Boroughs, Lawrence Chapel (early).

1867, Cane Creek, Eastatoe, 11 Mem. C. Roper.

1871, Eastatoe three churches, Cane Creek, Bethel, Whitesides.

1872, Flat Rock, (new), T. R. Gary.

1874, Easley, 20 Mem. J. C. Hudson, (Hunt's Memorial) (early).

1875, Prater's Creek, 15 Mem. J. H. Boroughs.

1878, Mile Creek, T. W. Tollison.

1878, Martin, J. T. Burdine.

1880, Pleasant Grove, W. A. Gidney Mt. Tabor (near Oolenoy.) 1882.

1880, Central, J. T. Lewis, Mt. Tabor (near Central) 1876.

1882, Four Mile Church, J. M. Stewart.

1886, Nine Forks, D. C. Freeman, (also) Camp Creek.

1889, Rocky Bottom, J. T. Burdine."

Other Baptist churches: Croswell, Cedar Rock, Rock Springs, Golden Grove, Golden Creek, Smith's Grove, King's Grove, Rice's Creek, Gap Hill, Glassy Mountain, Red Hill, Mt. Tabor, Mt. Sinai, Mountain View (1909), Faith Baptist church, Norris, Welcome, Fair View, Gates, and others.

OLD METHODIST CHURCHES

A tradition has been handed down in Pickens County that the oldest Methodist Churches, if not actually organized by Bishop Francis Asbury (the first Methodist Bishop in the United States), were at least the outgrowth of his preaching in this section. History tells us he traveled 275,000 miles on horseback.

This fact is verified by "Asbury's Journal", August 1771 to 1815. This Journal was published in three volumes 1821. It is now being published again.

Dated 1880, on page 2, Vol. 3 of his Journal, we read: "We had no small labour in getting down Seleuda (Saluda) Mountain, arriving at Father Douthat's on the south branch of the Seleuda River, where I had time to reflect on my western visitations."

And on page 3: "We have traveled about forty miles since we left Father Douthat's near Table Mountain, which on a clear day is a grand sight; the stool appears like a great house of free stone; today we saw it through a mist dimly. At the Cove there are few religious people."

On page 40, 1801: "We have been working this week from Seleuda to Reedy River, crossing and recrossing through Pendleton, Greenville, Laurens, and Newberry Counties in South Carolina."

1802, Page 85—"South Carolina, On Wednesday I directed my course to Solomon James's in the neighborhood of George's Creek, Pendleton County. I preached the funeral sermon of Polly James, the daughter of my host. Here I met with Major James Tarrant, a local preacher, riding the circuit."

1803, Page 120, "South Carolina; I rode to Chastain's twenty miles, crossing three branches of the Seleuda, not many miles from their source. Preached at the meeting house." (Probably Oolenoy).

Bethlehem Methodist Church near Pickens is known to have been organized soon after Polly James' funeral (1802). The Dacusville Methodist Church and Antioch (Methodist) were established about the same time, also Glassy Mountain Methodist Church (discontinued in the 1880's). Other old Methodist Churches in Pickens County, perhaps not as old as the first mentioned are: Tabor, Zion, Mt. Zion, Ruhama, McKinney's Chapel, Fairview, Perrit's Chapel, Gap Hill, New Hope, Union, Sharon, Twelve Mile, Salem, Porter's Chapel, Pickens; Easley; Liberty.

According to Dr. George Howe D.D., who wrote one of the early histories of the Presbyterian Church in South Carolina, old "Richmond" a log church located near the present site of the old Pickens Chapel graveyard, just over the Anderson County line was the first Presbyterian Church this far up-country in Ninety-six District. In old Presbyterial records "Richmond" is the first Presbyterian Church in the up-country to request supplies. This was about 1875.

Afterwards there was an unexplained confusion of names. In 1787 "Twenty-three Mile Creek", apparently near the same location applies for supplies. Richmond is not mentioned again, and Carmel is not mentioned as "Carmel" until 1793. But the first elders reported for Carmel are the same reported for Richmond and most of them are buried in the Pickens Chapel graveyard, which became a Methodist Church called "Pickens Chapel" after Robert Pickens bought a large plantation there which surrounded the old graveyard. "Twenty-three Mile Creek Church" was not mentioned again after Carmel. So, they must all be the same. Many Revolutionary soldiers are buried at Pickens Chapel.

RURAL NEEDS

A net-work of hard surfaced roads was spreading toward the back of the County and soon every farm house large and small had a TV arial. Someone remarked when we were riding that it was strange for people who couldn't afford comforatble homes to buy luxuries.

But is it strange? A man needs something uplifting in his life. This was brought to us forcibly several years ago. A friend and I were doing welfare work in a very humble home. We had prepared a baby for burial and placed it in a tiny casket, which stood on a box at the foot of the bed. There wasn't a chair in the house, the family sat on boxes; but in one corner of the room we noticed a large cabinet phonograph.

We looked at each other in amazement. And then the mother came into the room. She was old before her time and work-weary. She stood for a moment looking sadly at the baby's face. Then turning to us, she said: "Play 'Safe In the Arms of Jesus' ".

As the record played she stood and wept on the corner of her apron, and when the last note died away she told us: "That's the comfort in a music box. There's a tune for every feelin', sad or glad."

And now the pictures on TV are bringing the whole world into the most isolated homes. Uneducated people learn much they had not understood. They can even follow their boys in Service into strange lands overseas.

Chapter 16

From 1945 to 1958 Pickens County progressed rapidly. The consolidation of schools, the expansion of Farm and Home improvement was miraculous. Community Development Clubs were organized at Roanoke, Dayton, Crosswell, Twelve Mile, Oolenoy, Praters, and Maynard. There are thirteen Home Demonstration Clubs in the County for Farm Women, and twenty-two 4H Clubs for boys and girls.

All of the older cotton mills have built extensions and added modern machinery, most of them are under different management, because the first men have died or retired.

Many new plants have come to the County, Textron, Sangamo, Runnymede at Pickens, The Alexander Smith Rug Mill at Liberty. Elljean and Foster cotton mills came to Easley; and the big Saco Lowell Plant, among others already listed. Glenwood Mill, one of the first mills in the County was sold to the Mayfair Company and became "The Glenwood Division of Mayfair." The town of Easley spread in every direction, and its population was about 7000 in 1958.

Woodside No. 1 (often called the old Easley Mill) reached a million man hours for the third time without a lost time accident. A project to expand the weaving facilties of this mill has been approved by the president, Robert S. Small, to be accomplished in 1958.

The Central Mill has joined the Cannon Mill chain. A new bank opened in Central 1958, and a $1,000,000 plant for making piano parts was being built, called Pratt-Reed.

A new 100 bed hospital which cost Easley citizens $800,000 was dedicated June 29, 1958 and opened July'

1st. It is called "The Easley Baptist Hospital," with Mr. Wm. H. Coker, administrator.

The first Royal Ambassador Camp in the Southern Baptist Convention was being built (1958) fourteen miles north of Pickens on 120 acres of land, the gift of Mr. and Mrs. Roy McCall of Easley. This is in the Reedy Cove section of Pickens County.

The plans call for twelve cabins, a guest house, a staff house, an administration building, health building, activities building, chapel, and a craft hut. The cost of the camp, fully equipped, will amount to at least $300,000.

The Oolenoy Camp for children, in summer, with Miss Elizabeth Ellison in charge is located near Table Rock State Park. The Methodists are planning a camp near Caesar's Head.

Another camp that is creating county-wide interest, in the Oolenoy section of Pickens County, is called "The Greenville Rescue Mission Rehabilitation Farm." The farm was bought by the Greenville Rescue Mission in 1957. The Rev. Gerald Lehman, a graduate of Bob Jones University, and his wife are the 1958 Directors. It started with some old farm buildings and tents. Various types of under-privileged people have been kept for a period of weeks. The Florida truck growers in that section have been generous with donations of vegetables during the summer season, and the Oolenoy Community Center has shared their Community House for religious services.

The Oolenoy Community House is the former Oolenoy School House converted into a social hall for a community gathering place. By the untiring efforts of the Oolenoy women, with Mrs. J. I. Reece as leader, it has been remodeled inside and equipped for group entertaining, and they have added a picnic area and grills on the outside. This very oldest section of Pickens County may thus keep alive the Community Spirit of their pioneering ancestors.

190

The mill communities in Pickens County have good elementary schools. The Pickens Mill School was widely recognized over South Carolina under the leadership of Mrs. George Earle Keith as Principal. A great deal of Adult Education was sponsored by her. The Delegation was so impressed by the good work done in Adult Education in 1957-58 in Pickens County that they appropriated an extra $2000 for extension of the courses.

In 1958 several adult training classes were held at separate schools over the county for whites and negroes.

Pickens County negroes have good elementary and high schools, but these classes were for the underprivileged, adult part of the population. Adult classes for negroes were held at Clearview High School, Easley; the Pickens County Training School, Pickens; and the Calhoun Elementary School, Clemson.

Classes for white adults were held in various schools in the county.

School lunches have long been a part of the school program in Pickens County, Mrs. R. A. (Mozelle) Cole is the supervisor of this program.

There are active P.T.A. and P.T.O, and many youth organizations sponsored by the schools. Athletic clubs, music clubs, and literary clubs are a part of education in Pickens County.

Boy Scout training is county wide and they have had so many good leaders and so many interesting experiences that they could well write a book of their own. Troop 37 at Easley held the first Court of Honor in Pickens County in 1938. Scout Leader Jack Gantt of Pickens has done outstanding work, and other qualified leaders.

In the years between 1945-1958 many changes took place in the school system of Pickens County. Besides the new high school, already mentioned at Easley, there was a modern new half a million dollar high school built at Pickens to include the students from the upper part of the County, and Daniel High School was built to include the Central—Six Mile—Clemson area. New elementary schools were built at Holly Springs, Ambler, Martin-Prater, Six Mile, Clemson, Cateechee, Liberty, Easley, Croswell, and Dacusville.

One of the men who helped to make Clemson College a fine school was Dr. David Wister Daniel. He began teaching at Clemson College in his early youth, as an assistant professor of English, and then advanced to associate professor of English, Director of the Academic Department, Dean of Arts and Science Department, Dean of the School of General Science, and retired Dean Emeritus, and Profesor of English.

He was always a gifted speaker and many times through the years he has delighted Pickens County gatherings with his sparkling wit and humor.

It was very fitting that the new high school built between Six Mile and Clemson, and dedicated in 1956, should be named "The Daniel High school" in his honor, and the first school annual dedicated to him.

———————

Two natives of Six Mile who have helped Pickens County progress are Mr. John A. Roper, Sr., who still lives in Six Mile but has business interests all over the county, and Mr. Roy C. McCall who has become one of Easley's leading citizens.

Under a special law of 1935 an Agricultural Board was created for Pickens County and that was the beginning of soil conservation for this area. We are told that the late T. B. Nalley, of Easley, at that time a representatvie from Pickens County, instigated the measure, for Pickens County.

As the land became cleared much of the good soil washed away. The Twelve Mile Creek (River) water shed in the

Pickens area has begun a system of lakes and drainage designed to recover and reclaim much of the damaged property. Lewis E. Hendricks supervised the designing of this system.

Loblolly pines are being planted to help stabilize steep eroding and heavy sediment producing areas. 710,000 pines from the Piedmont Nursery were planted during 1957-58.

F. Guy Lindsey, Soil Conservationist at Pickens reported 2,772 acres of loblolly pines had been planted as a part of the project assistance, 1958.

Cotton production, once the leading source of money in Pickens County, decreased with the coming of the boll weevil and the curtailing of crops in the Roosevelt administration. The nearness to Clemson College gave the farmers an opportunity to study new experiments. The first truck load of pimentos left Pickens in August 1951, and a new side crop came into being. Other experiments followed until the farmers no longer depend on cotton. Many acres have been planted in grasses to raise sheep and cattle, and fruit growing, and poultry farms have become popular. Some of the mountain valleys are rented to Florida truck growers each summer who raise acres of small vegetables.

PIEDMONT NURSERY

In 1956 the State Forestry Department established the "Piedmont Nursery" in the northwestern part of Pickens County near Jocassee. This nursery is primarily for the purpose of furnishing pine seedlings to the farmers and woodsmen of Greenville, Anderson, Abbeville, Oconee, Pickens, Spartanburg, Cherokee, York, Chester, Fairfield, Newberry, and McCormick Counties who are interested in reforesting their land.

The location is ideal on account of good soil, and the eighty acres of land in the nursery is divided by the Eastatoe River which furnishes a good source of irrigation. The seeds

193

are planted in beds with a space of several seed beds between each irrigation pipe line. Various native trees will be raised in the seed beds.

The young plants are pulled from the ground by hand and placed in containers to be carried to the packing shed where they are processed into bundles for shipment. The bundles usually contain about 2000 plants.

Mr. Ernest Cooler, a 1941 graduate of Clemson, is in charge of the nursery in 1958, with a corp of four permanent workers, and forty or fifty community helpers in the harvesting season.

The first crop of the Piedmont Nursery was harvested in 1957 but the eighteen million seedlings failed to fill all of the orders that had come in. Reforesting with pines is a growing need in the South.

Among the forests of Pickens County there are various trees that have no commercial value and men engaged in forest research have studied methods to kill and replace them with more valuable trees. The County extension agents have secured one of the tree injectors to use in poisoning trees, that are undesirable.

In the 1940's Dwight A. Holder established a Memorial Park Cemetery on the Easley-Pickens Highway, and a little later another on the Easley-Liberty Highway.

Besides the town cemeteries long established, and a graveyard at every old church, there are many so-called family graveyards in Pickens County. Some of these are almost two hundred years old, and some have been neglected and forgotten until trees and brambles have grown over the sunken graves. A few of them are fenced and tended and are still being used for burial plots by descendants of our first settlers. The old family graveyards are too numerous to get an accurate record of them. A few of the best known ones are: Craig, Morgan, Norton, Baker, Day, McKinney, Boone-

Robertson, Head, Lewis, Hagood-Ambler-Griffin, Hunt, La-them, Easley, Turner, Hughes, Hester, Clayton, Stewart, Bowen, Mauldin, Kennemur, Hendricks, Oates, Barrett, Foster, Mayfield, Tally, Carpenter, Garrison, Hallum.

In the early 1950's the Pickens County Country Club was built in the center of the County. The low, rambling Club House is spacious and inviting and the cuisine is the best. There is an 18 hole golf course, tennis courts, and a swimming pool. The member-ship comes from all parts of the County and luncheons, receptions, and dinner parties are held there.

Besides the church, school, and farm organizations Pickens County has many that are civic and social: Masons, Eastern Star, Woodmen, Lions, Rotary, Jaycees, Medical Society, Medical Auxiliary, American Legion, American Legion Auxiliary, Veterans of Foreign Wars, D.A.R., S.A.R., U.D.C., Red Cross, Business and Professional Women, T.B. Association, Cancer, Polio, Muscular Dystrophy, Crippled Children, Air Corps Reserve, Historical Society, and others.

Grace Methodist Church, Pickens, burned in October 1945. Within the next four years a new church was built and dedicated, Sept. 25, 1949. A new parsonage had been built about 1940.

The Presbyterians in Pickens bought a manse and remodeled their church.

A new "Pickens Bank" was established in Pickens.

The Baptist church in Pickens built a new pastorium and an Educational Building. The Baptist Church at Griffin burned 1948 and they built a handsome church and pastorium, 1949.

A handsome new Baptist Church was built in Easley. The spirit of progress was abroad in the land and many improvements were made in churches over the County. Many of the old churches were brick veneered.

195

The old frame church at Oolenoy was torn down and a new brick church was built, with a pastorium near by. Some of the tombs in the ancient churchyard were restored, and a suitable marker bearing the Keith Coat-of-Arms was placed at the grave of Cornelius Keith, Sr., one of the first white settlers in Pickens County.

An Episcopal Church was established at Easley, the first of this denomination in Pickens County.

The Church of God first entered Pickens County in 1919. (Information obtained from the Rev. Wylie, Pickens Church through his church headquarters at Cleveland, Tenn.)

The first Church of God in the County was built near Central. In 1958 there are eleven orthodox Church of God Churches in Pickens County. There are others of various names not affiliated with the orthodox group. The officials of the Pickens Mill deeded a house on their premises as a church parsonage for their neighboring Church of God. (1958).

In 1951 Keowee Lodge No. 79 Ancient and Free Masons, which was organized at Old Pickens on Keowee River in 1851, celebrated its one hundredth anniversary at the Masonic Hall in Pickens.

Wyatt E. Durham, Master of the Lodge, displayed the one hundred year old Bible and the one hundred year certificate.

In 1951 there were twenty-five living Masters of the Lodge, and the following thirteen were present for the anniversary: J. E. Boggs, W. F. Welborn, R. R. Roark, Wyatt E. Durham, R. T. Hallum, Sr., B. H. Powers, J. O. Baker, George E. Welborn, S. W. Summey, T. C. Gravely, A. W. Bivens, W. T. Metts, R. T. Hallum, Jr., and Carlisle G. Durham.

Past Masters who were unable to be at the anniversary were: J. R. Ashmore, W. G. Lewis, Dr. J. L. Valley, Dr.

J. D. Yongue, J. T. Partridge, Dr. N. C. Brackett, C. C. Gillispie, W. S. Whitmire, Rev. B. S. Drennan, B. T. Winchester, W. C. Looper, and B. B. Porter.

In May 1958 W. L. Dowis, Sr., became the eighth living member of Lodge No. 79 AFM to receive a pin denoting fifty years of service as a member of the Masonic Order. Other members who have received fifty year pins include: W. McFall Baker, R. R. Roark, R. T. Hallum, Sr., J. W. Langston, J. T. Partridge, J. F. Williams, and D. Frank Hendricks.

Each Masonic Order sponsors an active Eastern Star group among the wives and daughters of members.

The Korean War took its toll of Pickens County boys.

Pvt. Charles H. Barker of Six Mile Community was another Congressional Medal winner. The medal was presented posthumously to his parents Mr. and Mrs. Norvin Barker, Route 1 Six Mile, in 1954, with suitable military honors.

Pvt. Charles H. Barker volunteered for the draft and took his basic training at Fort Jackson. He was a member of the 17th Infantry Regiment of the 7th Division. He was killed in action near Pork Chop Hill in Korea on June 4, 1953, while attempting to stop the advance of the enemy. Officials of the Army presented the Medal of Honor to his parents, and the Six Mile Community established a suitable marker in his memory. Many others were lost in battle.

Many who returned home had suffered sickness and wounds, with months of hospital treatment. Some had spent months in prison.

In September 1953 Corporal David E. Fortune, a Pickens County man, returned home after thirty-two months spent in a Red prison. Cpl. Fortune was a rifleman with Company E, 35th Infantry Regiment, 25th Infantry Division. He was captured near Seoul, Korea and marched three or four hundred miles with other prisoners. He saw some of his comrades die of starvation and disease, before the United Sttaes Government could get them released.

Pickens County Service Officer, T. N. Davidson, and Post 11 of the American Legion arranged an official welcome for Cpl. Fortune, and presented him a new car when he arrived in Pickens.

June 9, 1949 was an outstanding day in the lives of many Pickens County citizens when they honored their family doctor, John L. Valley. The tribute was paid to Dr. Valley at Table Rock State Park, and hundreds of people attended the picnic and the program, which for the most part consisted of expressions of praise and appreciation for Dr. Valley's long years of Service as a "family doctor" in upper Pickens County. There was much merriment over Dr. Valley's long procession of "babies", each wearing simulated baby caps, many of them men and women with families of their own.

Several gifts were bestowed upon Dr. Valley and members of his family, and last a bronze plaque bearing his likeness, and this inscription: "In honor of a great humanitarian, John L. Valley, M.D. Commemorating "Dr. Valley Day," June 1, 1949, Pickens, S. C., for his unselfish service with appreciation, love, and devotion from his friends."

Pickens County has been blessed with a number of good doctors. The first doctor in the bounds of the present Pickens County was Dr. John Robinson at Pickensville. His successors were Dr. Folger and Dr. Gilliland.

Easley's doctors have been: Dr. R. F. Smith, Jim Gilliland, Charles Wyatt, W. A. Tripp, C. M. Tripp, J. C. Pepper, Earl Russell, Edwin Wyatt, L. R. Poole, J. H. Cutchin, J. W. Potts, Wm. G. McCuen, J. A. White, J. Hal Jameson, E. A. Jamison, Robert P. Jeanes, Robert Merkle, C. F. Higgins, Dr. Bradley and others with the new hospital. (Veternarians) Dr. O. E. Ballenger, Dr. D. H. Spearman.

Dr. Francis Miles was the first doctor in Pickens. In a few years Mrs. Miles inherited the Caesar's Head Hotel and they moved there, spending each winter in Greenville. When they reached the age of retirement they deeded the Caesar's Head property to Furman University. They had no children.

Dr. George E. Earle was the second doctor in Pickens. He had a small drugstore, the first in Pickens, on the east end of Main Street. He was followed by Dr. Webb who owned the first automobile in Pickens. He named it "Della", and Della was often seen stranded on some country road. Other Pickens doctors have been: Dr. F. S. Porter, J. L. Bolt, J. A. Cannon, W. B. Furman, J. L. Valley, T. P. Valley, P. E. Woodruff, N. C. Brackett, Gaine Cannon, (who built the Cannon Clinic, and then enlarged it to a seventy bed hospital which he named "The Cannon Memorial Hospital" in honor of his father the late Dr. J. A. Cannon who had spent many years as a country doctor in our mountains.) Dr. Gaine Cannon also opened "The Lov'n Care Home" for elderly people. This closed in 1958 and "The Blue-Ridge Nursing Home" opened. Also the Harvey Home, Walhalla Highway.

Other Pickens doctors: Dr. John Harden, R. A. Allgood, Charles Ballard, Dr. Sydney Garrett, who has a clinic, his assistant Dr. Mann and others who only stayed in Pickens a short time, among them Dr. P. J. Moore, who now has a sanitarium at Fletcher, N. C.

Many years ago an old Dr. Grimshaw built a comfortable home in Eastatoe Valley and practiced medicine there. He was very fond of blood sausage, and he always killed his table chickens and placed them on the smokehouse roof until the feathers would pull easily. But he had the reputation of being a **fine doctor.**

Dr. Robert Kirksey practiced in the Crow Creek section of the County.

Six Mile had the great humanitarian Dr. David E. Peek,

who was a great physician with the added distinction of being the first to establish a hospital in Pickens County.

Liberty doctors have been: Dr. George Robinson (Confederate soldier)—Dr. Williams; W. A. Sheldon; W. M. Long; Walter M. Smith; Dr. Lucas; C. W. Smith; E. J. Bryson; A. Eugene Brown; P. E. Swords; M. J. Boggs; J. W. Kitchen, Dr. Charlotte Kay; William Hilton, Jr.; and his assistant Dr. Kennedy.

Central: Dr. Silas Clayton; Dr. Tom Folger; Dr. L. G. Clayton; Dr. J. D. Beardon; Dr. William Hunter.

Dacusville: Dr. J. A. Anderson; Dr. Morgan; and for many years Dr. William M. Ponder.

Pumpkintown: Dr. Bill Edens (Civil War days).

Pickens County Dentists: Dr. J. C. Walker, H. S. Williams, Frank B. Finley, J. Lloyd Garrison, J. D. Gillespie, Jr., Easley.

Pickens: Dr. Seawright, J. L. Aiken, Dr. Finley, B. R. Myers.

Liberty: Dr. D. H. Brown.

Undertakers: Robinson Company; J. Cliff Moore, Easley; J. M. Abbott, Robinson Company, J. J. Gantt, Liberty; Pickens, Guy McFall, Clayton-Dillard.

Some Pickens County Attorneys:

C. L. Hollingsworth, S. D. Goodlett, Norton & Hagood, W. K. Easley, (for whom the town of Easley was named because he was instrumental in getting the railroad at that location.) James P. Carey, Sr., J. E. Boggs, Sr., R. A. Child, W. E. Holcombe, R. E. Holcombe, T. J. Mauldin; I. M. Mauldin; W. E. Findley, Julien D. Wyatt; W. C. Mann, A D. Mann, Jr., James P. Carey, Jr., Lloyd Smith, Harris P. Smith, Sydney McDaniel, Felix L. Finley, John Gentry, John Vickery, W. G. Acker, George L. Grantham, W. A. Robinson.

In the early 1900's many covered bridges were built in Pickens County. In 1958 only Chapman's Bridge over the upper part of Keowee River remains.

The old grist mills, too, are disappearing along with the covered bridges. At least one of them should be preserved in good running order for the children of coming generations to see this most important item of the country's old time economy.

Our grandfathers liked to tell stories of going to mill in the old days, and as they talked you could almost see the clear sparkling water dashing along the mill race to turn the big wooden wheel that had a creaking sound all its own.

A few well known old mills in Pickens County were: Meece's, Calhouns', Symmes, Hunter's, Brown's, Kelly, Stewart, Lawrence, Craig, Boroughs, Smith, McKinney, Alexander, Nimmons, Winchester, Cantrell, Lynch, Reece, Price, Tally, Mayfield, Chastains, Gravely, Hagood, Clement, Mauldin, Kay, Curtis, Sheriff, Thomas, Hunt, Turner, Williams, and many others for there was at least one mill in every community.

Pickens County has a background of history and bright future prospects. There are occasional episodes that would furnish plots for current novels, but most of the citizens are real Americans interested in a Christian way of life.

Easley is the largest town in the County, but Pickens, the county seat located a little nearer the Blue Ridge Mountains, has the distinction of having the highest altitude of any town in South Carolina.

[END]

Table Rock

By

Mrs. Amos Sutherland
(Mrs. Sutherland was born and reared near Table Rock)

The first hotel at Table Rock was built about 1840 by William Sutherland. (It was located where the "Five Oaks" picnic area stands).

"The Sutherland family came from Virginia and settled in the lower part of Table Rock Cove on Saluda River, then moved to Oolenoy Valley and settled at a place that was later called Pumpkintown. William Sutherland was born February 6, 1788. On August 5, 1809 he married Sarah Keith. Her brother James Keith married Mary Sutherland, William's sister.

"They built a large two room house of logs with a corridor or entry between them and each family lived at one end. Later shed rooms were added and it became a wayside inn to accommodate travelers and tourists visiting this section.

"William Sutherland kept a stock of general merchandise while his brother-in-law James Keith farmed with slave labor. The fertile bottom land made great crops of corn, and pumpkins grew so large and plentiful that a wag called it "Pumpkintown."

"The supplies for the farm, store, and wayside inn were hauled from Augusta, Georgia in a wagon drawn by four horses. A slave named Jasper guided the four horses by placing the lines between the fingers of one hand in such a way only one hand was cold in winter. His fingers became stiff and drawn and remained that way as long as he lived.

"The produce sent to market was bacon, tobacco, and other farm products. Once William Sutherland ran out of feed for the horses before reaching home. He was out of cash. He bought feed from a man and promised to pay on his next trip down, which he did.

"The man told him to wait and pay as he came up. He replied: "As I go down I pay down, and as I come up I pay up."
Table Rock Hotel was built about 1840. The lumber was

sawed on a Pumpkintown farm. An upright or vertical saw was used as the circle saw was not common, or perhaps had not been invented at that time. After the hostelry was built William Sutherland moved his family to Table Rock and kept the hotel until his death which occurred January 22, 1859. The hotel was about seventy feet long by thirty feet wide, with wide verandas on each side and small bedrooms at the ends of these. The first floor had a large ballroom with a wide fireplace at one end and family living quarters at the other end, and an open corridor between the two. The living room had two bedrooms back of it. The second floor had a hall running lengthways with bedrooms on each side. There were about twenty rooms in all. The windows were small and the ceilings low, but whatever it lacked in architecture was made up for by the cool, bracing air and pure sparkling water of this delightful mountain region.

"A kitchen was set back of the house with fireplace and wide granite hearth. A crane on the side of the fireplace with iron pots and kettles suspended swung over the fire cooking pork, mutton, venison, hams, and sometimes wild turkeys or squirrel stew. The mountains at that time abounded in all kinds of game.

"The site chosen for the hotel was level and the front faced the great rock. Giant oaks grew in the yard, and a good spring was only a short distance at the foot of the mountain.

Tourists visiting Table Rock at that time often rode horseback up the steep ridge to the base of the rock. There in a little flat space between the base of the rock and the "Stool" Mountain was a place sometimes called the "Saddle" or the "Horserack." The horses were hitched there and the top of the rock reached by the steps.

The steps were built soon after the hotel was opened. A man named Daniel Carrol did the work. Holes were drilled in the rock, iron pins inserted and the steps bolted to the pins. The steps were in sections bridging the steepest points where there were no crevices or footholds by which one could climb. This was so much nearer than going up the trail on the western side. The great attraction on the trail route was the spring near the top. Around it grew "Hunter's Cups". They were green flowers shaped like small pitchers on shrubs, as if nature had provided a cup for the tired hunter to quench his thirst, after climbing the steep mountain.

On the top of the rock near the precipice a cedar, nourished by the soil washed against a ledge, grew out of a crevice in the rock until it became a tree. There was just enough space to walk between the tree and the edge of the precipice. It was a feat to boast of, going around the cedar tree. I have heard the story of a man from Charleston who stood on his head on a limb of the cedar tree. For lack of moisture and soil the tree died, and the top was broken off by the wind, but people continued to go around the stump until it was whittled away and carried off as souvenirs.

After the death of William Sutherland in 1859 the great Civil War came and there were not many visitors until the late seventies and eighties. Different ones own the place but it did not become popular again as a summer resort until Steven D. Keith took it over. Mr. Keith added noticeable improvements. A long two story ell was built, the first floor was used for a large dining room, pantry and kitchen. He also built a new barn for people had to travel in horse drawn vehicles and consequently needed a good place for the horses. After Mr. Keith's death the place was purchased by his nephew Nathaniel Keith, a bachelor, who lived there and rented rooms without meals. During the summer of 1897-98 the hotel was operated by Amos Coleman Sutherland and Frank E. Alexander. The summer of 1897 brought many tourists, but 1898 was a rainy season and owing to the condition of the roads there were few visitors. The house was badly in need of repairs at that time, but Mr. R. E. Chastain opened it for one year 1899.

A few years later E. Foster Keith built a new hotel nearer the base of the rock. It was well planned and located at a beautiful site on the side of the mountain. It had a spring nearby and a clear stream of water that dashed down the side of the mountain, and the yard was level with big shade trees. For a few years it had many visitors. Its only drawback was the steep, rocky road.

The hotel was sold and moved over into the Saluda Valley and made into a Club House. This was near the foot of beautiful Slicken Falls. Many visitors went to the Falls and bathed in the pool at the foot. When Greenville purchased the land in upper Saluda Valley for a reservoir the Club house was sold and moved out for a dwelling.

Efforts to make this a great playground were interrupted several times by wars in the century after the first hotel was built. The Civil War, the Mexican War, and the Spanish American War.

APPENDIX

Pickens, South Carolina (Pickens District) Chartered 1847

(Pickens Election District
Established under Act No. 4218, Acts of 1854)

1856-57:

    Senator:

    Representatives: James H. Ambler, James A. Doyle, John A. Easley, Jr.

1858-59:

    Senator: Elam Sharp

    Representatives: A. J. Anderson, George R. Cherry, Robert Maxwell

1860-61:

    Senator: Elam Sharp

    Representatives: M. Hendricks (probably Moses), Robert Maxwell, Jr.

1862-63:

    Senator: Robert Maxwell

    Representatives: J. A. Doyle, Morgan Harbin, Moses Hendricks, Samuel Lovinggood

1864: Journals burned by Sherman's Army

(From Miller's Almanac)

    Senator: Robert Maxwell

    Representatives: William S. Grisham, L. M. Robins, R. E. Bowen, R. E. Holcombe

Constitution of 1865

1865-66:

(Elected by lot)*

    Senator: William S. Grisham (Gresham*)*

    Representatives: R. E. Bowen, W. K. Easley, W. C. Keith, Jos. J. Norton

1867: No session

Constitution of 1868

1868-69:

    Senator: T. A. Rogers (by lot)*

    Representatives: William T. Field (Resignation accepted 1-5-69

1870-71:

    Senator: R. E. Holcombe

    Representatives: J. E. Hagood (son of Benjamin Hagood who established Caesar's Head Hotel.

1872-73:

        Senator: R. E. Holcombe

        Representatives: R. E. Bowen

1874-75:

        Senator: R. E. Bowen

        Representatives: D. F. Bradley

1876-77:

        Senator: R. E. Bowen

        Representatives: D. F. Bradley, Easley H. Bates

    *The name was originally Gresham. It is said that some schoolmaster mistakenly spelled it "Grisham" and some of the boys liked it and kept it that way.

    *Electing by lot was not uncommon when times were too unsettled to have regular political meetings.

1878-79:

        Senator: D. F. Bradley

        Representatives: W. I. Bowen, R. A. Child

1880-81:

        Senator: D. F. Bradley

        Representatives: J. C .Alexander, J. W. Tolleson

1882-83:

        Senator: W. T. Field

        Representatives: W. R. Berry, J. E. Boggs

1884-85:

        Senator: W. T. Field

        Representatives: J. E. Boggs, John H. Bowen

1886-87:

        Senator: W. T. Field

        Representatives: John A. Easley, B. J. Johnson

1888-89:

        Senator: W. T. Field

        Representatives: J. H. Bowen, B. J. Johnson

1890-91:

        Senator: W. T. O'Dell

        Representatives: W. T. Bowen, C. H. Carpenter

1892-93:

        Senator: W. T. O'Dell

        Representatives: C. H. Carpenter, Laban Mauldin

1894-95:

        Senator: W. T. O'Dell

        Representatives: B. J. Johnson, Fred Williams

1897-98:

        Senator: W. T. O'Dell

        Representatives: W. G. Mauldin, Joel H. Miller

1899-01:
Senator: W. T. Bowen
Representatives: Laban Mauldin, C. E. Robinson
1901-02:
Senator: W. T. Bowen
Representatives: Ivy M. Mauldin, C. E. Robinson
1903-04:
Senator: C. H. Carpenter
Representatives: Matthew Hendricks, J. A. Hinton
1905-06:
Senator: C. H. Carpenter
Representatives: Laban Mauldin, T. J. Mauldin
1907-08:
Senator: C. H. Carpenter
Representatives: J. P. Carey, J. A. Hinton
1909-10:
Senator: C. H. Carpenter
Representatives: J. P. Carey, W. G. Mauldin
1911-12:
Senator: Thos. J. Mauldin
Representatives: W. G. Mauldin, E. P. McCravy
1913-14:
Senator: Thos. J. Mauldin (resigned when appointed
Judge)
Representatives: E. P. McCravy, Fred Williams, J. L.
Bolt (Sworn in 1-13-1914)
1915-16:
Senator: W. T. O'Dell
Representatives: J. L. Bolt, J. P. Carey, Jr.
1917-18:
Senator: W. T. O'Dell
Representatives: W. E. Findley, W. Luther Pickens
1919-20:
Senator: Frank E. Alexander
Representatives: Jesse S. Leppard, W. C. Mann
1921-22:
Senator: Frank E. Alexander (died 8-26-21)
E. P. McCravy sworn in 1-10-22
Representatives: J. S. Leppard, J. O. Williams
1923-24:
Senator: John E. Craig
Representatives: W. E. Findley, J. O. Williams
1925-26:
Senator: John E. Graig

207

Representatives: W. E. Findley, J. O. Williams
1927-28:
Senator: W. E. Findley
Representatives: John P. Smith, W. D. Spearman
1929-30:
Senator: W. E. Findley
Representatives: C. L. Cureton, J. Mack Jameson
1931-32:
Senator: W. D. Spearman
Representatives: J. Austin Dillard, T. B. Nalley
1935-36:
Senator: Fred F. Williams
Representatives: J. Drufus Griffin, T. B. Nalley
1937-38:
Senator: Fred F. Williams
Representatives: J. T. Black, W. B. Davis
1939-40:
Senator: Fred F. Williams
Representatives: G. M. Perry, G. Milton Ponder
1941-42:
Senator: Fred F. Williams
Representatives: John R. McCravy, Thomas B. Nalley
1943-44:
Senator: Fred F. Williams
Representatives: Ben T. Day, G. M. Perry
1945-46:
Senator: Fred F. Williams
Representatives: T. B. Nalley, G. M. Perry
1947-48:
Senator: T. B. Nalley
Representatives: Dwight A. Holder, Theron P. Kelly
1949-50:
Senator: T. B. Nalley (died 6-15-50)
Representatives: Dwight A. Holder, John D. Vickery,
Jr.
1951-52:
Senator: Geo. L. Grantham
Representatives: Earle E. Morris, Jr., Ben F. Under-
wood
1953-54:
Senator: Geo. L. Grantham
Representatives: Earle E. Morris, Jr., John T. Gentry

1955-56:
        Senator: Earle E. Morris, Jr.
        Representatives: Harold D. Breazeale, John T. Gentry
1057-58:
        Senator: Earle E. Morris, Jr.
        Representatives: Harold D. Breazeale, John T. Gentry

        Pickens County Offiicals (State Library, Columbia)
                            1868-1958
        Clerk of Court
R. A. Bowen 1868-1872
S. D. Keith 1872-1876
J. J. Lewis 1876-1888
J. M. Stewart 1888-1900
Aaron J. Boggs 1900-1916
O. S. Stewart, 1916-1932
B. T. McDaniel, 1932-34
E. P. McDaniel, 1934-1958

        Sheriff
Joab Mauldin, 1868-72; 1876-84. Deputy, Riley Ferguson
1868-72
Riley Ferguson, 1872-76
Joab Mauldin (second term 76-84)
H. A. Richey 1884-1892
J. H. G. McDaniel 1892-94
J. C. Jennings 1904-1908
R. R. Roark, 1908-1924
John B. Craig, 1924-1934
Andy R. Ross, 1934-1940
Waymond H. Mauldin, 1940-1948
P. Clyde Bolding, 1948-

        Treasurer
W. M. Lesley, 1868-69; removed Aug. 11, 69; 1870-75
W. R. Berry, 1875-77
T. W. Russell, 1877-78
B. F. Morgan, 1879-81
J. H. Bowen, 1881-84
John Tyler Hill, 1884-91
John T. Youngblood, 1891-1901
Samuel D. Chapman, 1901-1903
Henry W. Farr, 1903-1907
B. D. Garvin, 1907-1911

James T. Richey, 1911-1912
J. H. Stewart, 1912-1917
Olar T. Hinton, 1917-1925
Jesse D. Gillispie 1925-1958

Auditor
H. M. Folger, 1968- removed August 11, 1869; 1869-1875
Alonzo M. Folger, 1875-77
J. Frank Folger, part of 1877
John A. Davis, 1877-78
W. H. Hester, appointed (not confirmed by Senate).
Waddy T. McFall, 1879-1881
J. B. Clyde, 1881-1893
W. H. Bryant, 1893-95
N. A. Christopher, 1895-1899; 1907-1917
Samuel A. Hunt, 1899-1901
E. Foster Keith, 1901-1907
Henry A. Townes, 1917-1928
A. J. Boggs, Jr., 1929-1937
R. C. Griffin, 1937-
Wyatt E. Durham

Supervisor
Matthew Hendricks, 1894-1896
W. P. Looper, 1896-1900
Leonard D. Stephens, 1900-1904
Gideon M. Lynch, 1904-1906
James B. Craig, 1910-1919
J. T. McKinney, 1919-1930
Geo. H. Hendricks, 1930-1934
T. Ross O'Dell, 1934-
Guy Nealy

Judge of Probate
Irvin H. Philpot, 1868-1876
W. G. Field, 1876-1878
O. L. Durant, 1878-1882
J. H. Newton, 1882-1886
J. B. Newberry, 1886-1896; 1897-1900; 1902-1921
N. A. Christopher, 1921-1922
R. A. Hudson, 1922-1934
E. A. Lewis, 1934-1958

Coroner
Thos. S. Roe, 1869-1872
Warren Boyd, 1872-1876
B. B. Earle, 1876-1878
Thos. Parkins, 1878-1880
O. K. Kirksey, 1880-1884
Since 1936
J. A. Leslie, 1884-1888
P. H. Boggs, 1888-1892; 1908-10
W. S. Parsons, 1892-97
W. D. Jones, 1897-1900
Ben F. Parsons, 1900-1904
B. F. Dorous, 1901
D. A. Parrott, 1904-1908
Millard F. Hester, 1910-1911
Joe E. Medlin, 1911-1919
Oscar Durham, 1919-1921; 25-28
W. T. Beasley, 1921-25; 1928-36
D. H. Ramsey, 1936
Clement Smith

Superintendent of Education:
Note: Before the present Pickens County was established,
(1868) In 1850, the General Assembly appointed a board of sev-
en free School Commissioners for Pickens District for a term of
three years.

In 1868 the Constitution provided for one School Commissioner elected biennially by the electors of the County. He was
a member, ex-officio of the State Board of Education, and a
member of the County Board to examine applicants for teaching. He appointed two men to assist him.

In 1896 a County Superintendent of Education replaced
these men, and a County Board of Education was appointed.
Several other changes have been made through the years.

Superintendents of Education:
J. K. Riley, 1896-1899
W. W. F. Bright, 1899-1903
Richard T. Hallum, Sr., 1903-1917
F. Van Clayton, 1917-18; 1921-1925
George E. Welborn, 1925-1937
Edwin L. Bolt, 1937-
E. S. Craig (died in office)
W. Frank Welborn, 1937-1957
J. E. Ponder, 1957

211

1958-1959 BOARD OF EDUCATION

Mr. James E. Ponder, Chairman . . . Dacusville
Mr. E. Wayne Williams, Secretary . . Dacusville
Mr. J. B. Childs . . . . Central
Mr. E. M. Duncan . . . . . . Six Mile
Mr. George W. Goldsmith . . . . . Liberty
Mr. Tom S. Milford . . . . . . Clemson
Mr. J. Lake Williams . . . . . . Easley

ACKNOWLEDGEMENTS

We do not offer this as a complete history of Pickens County, for that would take many volumes.

The historical facts are true to the best of our research and ability. They are taken from the oldest South Carolina records in Charleston, Columbia, Greenville and Clemson College Libraries.

Adair, Mooney, Lawson, Hewitt, Ramsey, Logan, Robert Mills and many old manuscripts, court records and letters were the sources we used.

Later facts came from privately owned files of newspapers, and from State and National pamphlets dating back to the 1860's.

We gratefully acknowledge facts and pictures from the following: Mrs. J. I. Reece, Pumpkintown, Mr. C. C. Boroughs, and Miss Carrie Hutchins, Liberty, S. C., Dr. J. L. Valley, Miss Jewell Henderson, and Mrs. Jessie Clement, Pickens, S. C., Mrs. D. E. Peek, Six Mile, Mrs. J. A. Dillard, Pickens.

And we are deeply indebted to: Mr. Glenn A. Cannon, Columbia, S. C. for hand drawn sketches of some of the old grist mills, and of Piedmont Institute the first High School in Pickens County.

And also to Johnny Joe Davis, president of the student body of Pickens High School 1958, for the sketch of Pickens County on the cover of the book.

INDEX

6770